MUSTANG

MUSTANG

RICHARD CARLYON

CP

Additional editorial material supplied by Tony Beadle

This revised edition published in 1989
Chevprime Limited
27 Swinton Street, London WC1X 9NW

ISBN 1 85361 060 7

Printed in Italy

CONTENTS

CHAPTER 1

HOW IT ALL BEGAN

Previous page: The Mustang that hit the roads.

In the beginning there was Lee Iacocca. In the beginning there was the 221 Fairlane thin-wall engine, and a multitude of young drivers about to come onto the market. And Ford looked out and saw the obvious, and Ford realized they could be onto a winner and Ford said, 'Let there be a car for the multitudes to buy. Let it be stylish, muscular and with the right price tag. But let it be soon, damn soon, before GM and the others get there before us.' And the countenance of Ford shone upon Lee Iacocca and Ford proclaimed, 'Go to it, Lee baby!' And Lee went to it. And after much travail behold, there was the Mustang.

Well, it wasn't quite like that, but after a while every great event becomes shrouded in myth.

In 1955 the Thunderbird was launched, followed in 1958 by the four-seat Thunderbird. They were both heavy cars, constructed round the great powerhouse of the Ford high-performance V8 engine. The weight of the engine, and its size, meant that the Thunderbird was no chicken, and its consequent price put it into the luxury bracket. Ford had the age-old problem of producing a sporty, powerful package at a tag affordable by the young drivers. Sales of imported small cars were booming and so Ford put their effort into the economical, trusty new car named Falcon. It sold nearly half a million in its first year and a million in its second year. Somehow, between the mighty Thunderbird and the plain Falcon, there was a car waiting to be built, a car that was powerful but not for the rich only, a car that was small but not for the timid family man, a sporty car not necessarily a sports car, a neat package of easily-handleable power with a stylish image.

Ford's first problem was that it did not have a clear theme for the gap in its product line-up. Lee Iacocca's promotion to lead the Ford Division brought a man with youth and ideas into the right spot. He was a man who loved the Thunderbird and its looks. The T-bird had a long hood, short deck and low roofline. The T-bird was to be the true starting point for the car that Ford's heavy research had told them they must have. The car had to be new, exciting and powerful, also small (180 in), light (2500 lb) and inexpensive ($2500). It had to carry four and be adaptable to a variety of tastes. Research into what young drivers wanted indicated a variety of items found in imported sports cars, power, agility, bucket seats, and floor-positioned gear-shifts. Ford had also noticed that even buyers of economy models like the plain Falcon wanted optional automatic transmission, white-wall tires, bigger engines and such. As Iacocca was to observe: 'People want economy so badly they don't give a damn how much they pay for it.' GM had already led the way by sprucing up its dull Corvair with stylish optionals and calling it the 'Monza'.

Ford ran a marketing test which confirmed that there were people out there eager to buy the kind of car Ford had in mind, and the age group of 18–34 would soon be responsible for buying half of the new cars in the 1960s. Iacocca was fretting to hit this huge potential market before anyone else. Ford took a first step by introducing the Falcon *Sprint*. It was the basic economy car but with added bucket seats, floor shift, a new roof that harked back to the Thunderbird and, most important of all, the 221 Fairlane V8. It sold well, reinforcing Iacocca's conviction that the new car had to hit the streets as soon as possible.

Ford styling chief Gene Bordinat was assigned to line up Ford cars against the other available types of car on the market. Ford had nothing to put up against the Monza.

Now every car designer (like every writer and every composer) has a few outlines of things he would like to do, which he keeps by, just in case. Bordinat was no exception. He brought out a design called Allegro, a secretly-concocted car plan including all the design items that Iacocca immediately responded to. The Allegro was not right, but it proved that the long hood, short deck and low-roof features could be brought together successfully in the kind of design format needed. The designers were told to go ahead along those lines. At the same time Iacocca was trying out the idea of bringing back the original Thunderbird, by taking the two-seater and making a four-seater from it; what came out of this effort was still a two-seater, the XT-Bird, but with strong Falcon looks. It was rejected as being too expensive and also it did not meet the four-seat requirement.

The design package was eventually put out on a competitive basis to Corporate Projects, Ford, and Lincoln-Mercury. A race-track atmosphere hit the corporation as designers locked themselves away, refusing their former friends any glimpse of their own ideas.

The competition was fierce and spirited and it produced a variety of remarkable designs which were all solutions to the problem which had been posed.

When the designs were reviewed, a car called the Stiletto was much in favor; but it was costed out and found to be too expensive to produce. The other favorite, which displayed the traditional Ford features (found in the Thunderbird and Lincoln Continental II) of roofline and outline, was a small dynamic-looking vehicle named the Cougar. The Cougar, later renamed the Mustang, found such approval among engineers and designers that it went from clay full-size rendering to the assembly line with fewer changes than anyone had ever experienced in a car.

The date was Fall 1962 and Iacocca was still scaling the tiresome heap of meetings and reports that had to be ascended before Ford top management would give him the final go-ahead. Cost was the main problem. Ford was into heavy reinvestment and the accountants were focussing on the dollars needed to produce the Cougar profitably. In the back of everyone's mind was the ghost of the Edsel; like this new car it too had been heavily researched and all the signs had, on paper, pointed to success.

Iacocca had two good arguments. Because of compatible Falcon components the time and investment in tooling was shortened. The other argument was that Henry Ford II liked the car. Iacocca was given a 'yes,' a budget of $40 million and a seemingly impossible production schedule of 18 months before the first new sporty car rolled off the end of the production line at Dearborn, the first of a planned volume of 75,000 units.

Interestingly, at the time of Iacocca's go-ahead, there was already a Ford Mustang being built. It was to be wheeled out complete only a matter of two weeks or so after Iacocca's successful presentation. It was this car, not the Dearborn production model, that achieved the distinction of being called *Mustang One*.

CHAPTER 2

THE MUSTANG RACER

In 1957 the Automobile Manufacturers' Association banned the involvement of manufacturers in racing in a general attempt to divert emphasis from performance and power in production cars. In the NASCAR and USAC stock circuits, Ford had been a leading name, and was now to lose its predominance speedily. Ford executives could do nothing but complain since they had a good idea that several of their competitors were still involving factory time, money and parts in racing. They attributed GM success to this back-door activity. It is fair to note that GM executives were thinking the same about their competitors, including Ford. What was interesting, and the reason why it is mentioned here, was the part all this played in the generating of the 'ponycar' concept. Finally Ford had had enough and declared openly that they too were going into racing with heavy sponsorship. It should be noted here that Ford had actually been toying with racecar plans and had already taken an interest in Carroll Shelby's experimental idea of taking the sleek English AC racer and putting a Ford 260 V8 engine into it. The result was the Cobra, which was tested in 1962. Shelby's idea won him a contract with Ford, who received immediate benefit in the widespread media interest surrounding the new car.

Ford had also formed an association with Dan Gurney and Colin Chapman, renowned producer of the Lotus. Gurney and Chapman had the idea that a rear-engined car might very well win the grueling Indianapolis 500 if only they could get hold of the right engine. They approached Ford, who had had the same idea, a lightweight, tough engine of about 350 horsepower. They were welcomed into the club.

There were two devoted private teams running Fords,

Holman-Moody with ace driver Fred Lorenzen, and the Wood Brothers. Ford was building up a talented group of allies.

Not long before this there had almost been a car called 'Cardinal,' a project which in Germany was later successful as the 'Taunus.' It had front-wheel drive and other sophisticated concepts under a plain, boxy body. From this drivetrain emerged the idea for a lightweight sports car, a car with a difference since the engine would be *behind* the two seats. Nothing came of this idea at first, but later when everyone was thinking mid-engine, the concept was to bear fruit. Stylists John Najjar and Jim Sipple came up with a small race car using the Cardinal drivetrain. It was beautiful. It was quickly authorized and in an amazing five months a functional prototype was ready for public viewing at Watkins Glen. How did they do it? An executive visited the Ford plant in Cologne and to his great surprise 'found they had built one transaxle too many.' By some strange coincidence, the Cardinal prototype shop had also 'made one engine too many.' How fortunate. In addition there were several private firms working flat-out to deliver various parts to specification.

The car was small, and had a front like an axe blade, louvered air vents fore of the rear wheels to provide breathing for the rear-mounted engine and a spoiler-type roll bar. It also had a name that was to become famous – Mustang. The name referred to the World War II fighter plane, but it was also full of connotations of wildness, power, open plains and historic pioneer days. The designers emphasized its American nature by placing red, white and blue bars behind a design of a running pony.

Apart from being a great-looking sports car, the *Mustang I* had all the required items for everyday street use; concealed

Previous page: With racing in their blood, Mustangs like these at Le Mans were natural competitors on the track.

Below: A cutaway view of the '64 V8 shows the robust construction.

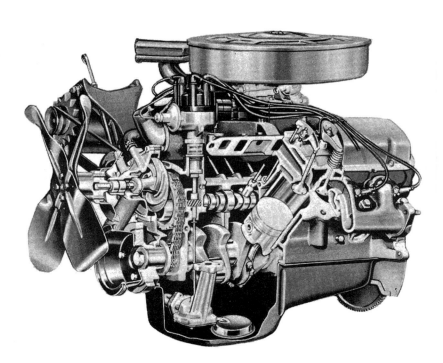

headlamps, faired-in parking and rear lights and provision for front and rear license plates. Its 1.5-liter V4 engine was uprated to 109 hp by higher compression, it had a special-design intake manifold, tough camshaft and dual Weber carbs, hydraulic clutch, and its console-mounted gear shift connected to the four-speed axle by control cables. Racing suspension was integral coil spring/tube shock-absorbers; at the rear were coil-over shocks and trailing strut rods on a tubular A-frame. Front disk and rear drum brakes had dual master cylinders.

In the cockpit the seats were fixed, so the steering column and pedals were made adjustable instead, a very neat achievement; battery, spare tire and fuel tank were up front. Dual exhausts ducted emission from each 2-cylinder bank through a transverse muffler and on through dual pipes out of the rear panel. The whole emission system was mounted on the transaxle-engine unit.

Mustang I was a car that could have gone into production if the decision had ever been forthcoming. It was more than just a sports car. Its designers were proudly able to compare it to all the main European imports. The only comparison missing was that of price.

What was not missing at the Watkins Glen unveiling of *Mustang I* was excitement and wide public acclaim. Dan Gurney drove the car round the Grand Prix course, and it caused a sensation! A flood of enthusiastic press reports followed after journalists had been allowed to test-drive the car, some of them in its street trim. Ford had not seen such public enthusiasm for a long time, and the new sports car caught a large amount of valuable front page coverage for the Corporation. Public enthusiasm for the car was kept up by a touring road show, while a non-functional fiberglass copy was duplicating the effect in showrooms and public places. But it was never to see production. Even as it was drawing admiring crowds, Fords were at work developing the mid-engine concept in the direction of the Ford GT 40 racing car. The original was saved from the destructive intentions of various managers by three designers who fought a long and secret battle to preserve the car. After 14 years they decided to hand it over to the Ford Museum.

Throughout all those years they had hoped that the car would one day go into production. But it was not to be. It had done its job of attracting the public's attention to Ford's new style of car, and to Ford's new philosophy of youthful good looks, imaginative styling and ease of handling. Iacocca knew he had a huge market out there waiting for the right kind of car. He now had a good design, the Cougar, and a lot of buzz about a good name – Mustang.

Above: '64 convertible.

CHAPTER 3

MUSTANG FOR THE ROAD

Even if the Ford design and engineering team had had more than the year-and-a-half schedule to put the road Mustang into production from a set of drawings and a clay model, it seems unlikely they would have made any drastic changes.

Of course there was a lot of work to be done on the detail, especially the interior instrumentation and trim, but body-wise and engineering-wise the car was just about there from the beginning.

David Ash, who had put together the design in the absence of his boss Joe Oros, had given the car oblong headlamps which had to be replaced by round lamps, because of Federal regulations. The distinctive recessed panel, which in the *Mustang I* served the essential purpose of sucking in air to the mid-mounted engine, was straightened a mite to ease the production processes.

But at this moment there were other things apart from a design that won universal approval, other things that were of incalculable benefit in creating the success story that the Mustang was destined to narrate across the roads, turnpikes and streets of the States, and indeed across the cinema and tv screens of the whole world. The first advantage was Lee

The '63 Mustang prototype, in the tradition of concept cars for public viewing, formed a link between the small racing car unveiled previously and the production Mustang.

1965 Mustang convertible.

Iacocca, a burly but sensitive man who was prepared to put his meteoric career of success on the line over this one product. Iacocca was courageous in the teeth of sharp opposition from a continuing corps of highly placed doom-mongers at Dearborn. Later we shall see the lengths he went to to make the Mustang dream come true. Then there was the unity of design that aroused the admiration and respect of all who were involved, either at first hand or by other formal connections. Designers, modellers, engineers, writers, artists, advertising men, marketing and promotion men, managers, researchers and finally the great public were all involved

with what can fitly be described as a love affair with an epoch-making concept. The designers especially stood by their baby, guarding it from all the threats that are constantly around when engineers and accountants try to save inches and dollars by small but important compromises of design.

Another great asset was the fact that in the giant waterfall of effort, creativity, organization, engineering and money-handling that was the Ford Corporation, the Mustang was a small enterprise by comparison with other more costly projects. None of the big guns thought it worth their while to

Many of the production details. such as the rear lights. were worked into the showcar as previews of the consumer model.

The unmissable recessed scoop of the Mustang was to be a trademark for many years. The final Mustang was squarer than this showcar. as it had to accommodate itself to the realities of mass production.

range in on the Mustang project; in fact this was sometimes a danger, for the project was frequently called into question as being not worth doing at all. These dangers Iacocca had to fight with research, and research, and yet more research.

Also working for the project was something that could have been seen as a danger: the fact that only 18 months were available before the first street unit was to be completed.

It is probably true to say that quite a lot of Ford people, who

were not directly connected with the project, at first may have considered the whole thing bound for a quite modest level of viability. This was to cause problems since the Mustang team relied on other Ford departments for the production of essential trial components.

The outside of the car presented only minor problems, although there was a design doubt about the prominence of the high, mouthy grille opening. Iacocca wanted to achieve the protruberant 'growly' look and this meant that a lot of delicate but practical fiddling-about had to be gone through. Various combinations of grille and lights were tried out, and at this stage the car was still being called the Cougar. T5, Special Falcon and Torino were other names seriously tried,

Lee Iacocca takes the wheel of the Mustang showcar while Graham Hill takes a back seat.

all with motifs which appeared on the grille. There were also several different horse designs for the Mustang, with the designers remembering the black prancing horse motif of the legendary Ferrari. The 'father' designers of the Mustang, Dave Ash and Joe Oros, pushed hard for the name Cougar. They were to be disappointed, but their name and cat designs were later to be used for a different car. Iacocca has been quoted as saying, 'Picking a name is the toughest part of making a new car. It gets very emotional at times.' A lot of research˙ was done, and these surveys favored the name *Mustang*. This name had of course been used for the two-seat rear-engine showcar, a car with the strikingly similar side recessed panel. It began to make some sort of design sense,

and this was to be cleverly followed up by another public teaser, the showcase *Mustang II*. But before going into that, we should return to the design and engineering story of the production car itself.

There were to be three interiors, each with its own feel: a base interior that had to be clean and functional; a sports-style interior that had to give the feel of the well-machined, precision style of top European sports cars; and a luxury job that pampered the driver with its feeling of exclusivity. The instrument panel followed the Falcon style with cluster panel and optional gauges of rally-styling on each side of the wheel. The inner door panels were an innovation, made of stamped sheet metal and textured to an attractive softness. A lot of different designs were considered for the switches, keys and functional handles to get the right shape and material and to give the right feel. A big problem was discovered in the relationship between the seating and the accelerator pedal. Test drivers noted an uncomfortable match, resulting in ankle fatigue. It was only solved late in the program by relocating both seat and pedal, and by trying variations to discover the best angle at which the pedal and pedal pad should relate to the driver.

In an attempt to give the car extra appeal, a removable· hardtop and a fiberglass tonneau were designed, but their manufacturing cost made them dead-ends. It was in things like this that the limitations of the program were shown. Another great limitation was that the engineers working on the Cougar/Mustang had to rely on the separate Ford divisions for their components, having to go to the Engine division for their engines, and so on. Without the components they were stuck, because they first had to build prototypes, test them and make the necessary changes in the components for the final production build. Once they asked the Transmission and Axle division for eight different rear axles to try out various ratios. After refusals based on lack of financial authorization, the Axle division finally agreed to supply two out of the eight required axles. The Exhaust division refused to help with the exhaust designs at all and so two engineers on the project, C Reuter and Jack Prendergast, were compelled to work late at nights designing the exhaust systems on borrowed designers' tables (after the designers had gone home for the night). That is the sort of devotion the car inspired in the group. Incidentally, the two engineers came up with a completely new design concept for the exhaust; they mounted the muffler transversely under the rear pan. They did this simply because it seemed to them the best way of solving a problem they had never encountered before.

A lot of Falcon components were used, either as they were or with minor modifications to suit the smaller size of the new car. These modifications had to be subtle enough to suit the unique character of the sporty Mustang but not great enough to require expensive retooling for altogether new components.

They used the Falcon suspension with a little tightening here and there and changed the steering linkage of the Falcon to accommodate the V8 and to make the handling that more sensitive. Of course some things had to be different. The new car was lower and wider than the Falcon; the lowness meant that the floor had to be made lower, thus requiring a higher central tunnel for the existing Falcon drivetrain. This in fact turned out to be quite suitable as the new car was destined to have bucket seats only. With the seats lower, they could bring down the roof as well and achieve the sleek sporting image they desired. They brought the hood down as close to the engine as possible, giving it sculptured lines which were purely functional and therefore honest and effective.

They also came up with a new construction idea that was to save money and weight. This was to eliminate the structural torque box of the Falcon floor pan by tying the structure of the transmission tunnel up into the dashboard panel and forward windshield pillars.

The team soon acquired a strong spirit of togetherness and determination and even began to wear identification pins to indicate their functional fraternity. As Reuter says, 'We weren't going to take "no" from anybody!'

They fought hard to get what they needed, and even harder to get what they wanted, and they built a prototype that came in *under* the allocated weight and under the allocated price tag.

When they took the new car out on test trips they caused havoc! Crowds numbering hundreds gathered when they stopped to eat, their motel was besieged by eager young drivers who kept them awake until two in the morning with their noisy enthusiasm for the strange, exciting new car. They were chased and flagged down by men determined to buy the car from them. They protested that it was a prototype costing over $100,000 and one man wanted to buy it even at that price!

Even more research was mounted by the still eager Iacocca (who was still justifying his project to top Ford management) and the research showed that people expected to pay in the $3500–$3800 bracket for the new car. Some people put the price of the car way up in the Ferrari level, over $7000.

A group of standard family-car buyers were shown the car and all overestimated the price. When they learned the expected price, their previous lack of interest in buying it vanished like mist in the summer sun. Instead of stating why they would *not* buy it, they began stating why they *would* buy it.

As the car looked more and more likely to be a winner, all the people who had refused help to the team began offering all the help they could give. Wider enthusiasm in Ford itself resulted in Iacocca approaching higher management and asking for increased production volume. Despite the fact that the project had begun small, they agreed, pausing only to point out to Iacocca that it was his decision. In effect they were saying that his whole career was on the line. Iacocca's confidence never wavered. As he said: '. . . You have to make up your mind.'

The original planned volume was 75,000 units. It grew to 200,000. Another plant was tooled-up to give a possible volume of 360,000 units per year. As the car was being introduced, yet another plant was being equipped to produce yet more Mustangs per year.

Iacocca himself was aware of another danger, that of

Known as the 64½ Mustang, this convertible was one of just under half a million sold in the first sales year.

Opposite: Power and comfort were the keynotes of the interior of the Mustang.

From the first, the Mustang was publicly honored. The '64 model was chosen to pace the Memorial Day Indy 500.

making too few cars to satisfy the demand. This had happened with the Falcon and he was not going to succeed so well that success became a failure and people began taking him to task for under-production. But it took nerves of steel to ask for such a huge increment in annual units on a car that had not even been introduced.

It has already been said that the designers and engineers had put the Mustang together under the cost ceiling. Ford now took advantage of this to make the car even more appealing. People were used then to buying base cars and, since the price had already been set at $2368, Iacocca put in what he fondly describes as 'cues,' those little touches which signal the sort of style people crave. These were full wheel covers instead of dinky little hubcaps, bucket seats, carpeting, padded instrument panel, cigarette lighter — things that were considered extras were now included for the base price.

Another excellent marketing approach was to resist the temptation of giving the more powerful, fully-optioned models a spurious separate identity. This was usually done by tagging them with an 'exotic' foreign name or by calling them after a racetrack or race, trying to acquire a dimension to which they were in all honesty not entitled. The Mustang was to be the Mustang, whichever of the three models you chose.

Iacocca was the first to admit that he and his designers were taking risks, steering their car between the bland sedan and the fire-breathing dragon on wheels. Both of these extremes were a turn-off for the market they wanted to capture. Another important job was still to be done before the Mustang could be revealed; public interest had to be jerked into awareness. That was to be the job of the Mustang II, a car designed to be a signal for the production Mustang.

CHAPTER 4

MUSTANG MANIA

The Mustang II was purely a show car, an attention-getter, a bridge-builder between the racer and the street Mustang. There was no clear connection between the two, so Ford created one, mindful of the flood of publicity success they had achieved with the Mustang I at Watkins Glen. Iacocca later stated that it was built to test public reaction but to tell the truth it was more to provoke or create reaction. It was unveiled to universal admiration six months before the launch of the production Mustang. It was close to the final Mustang but with carefully added cues from the racer, a longer front coming to a distinctive edge, no fenders, roll-bar and very stylish front and rear lights.

It got a lot of coverage, preparing people for what was to come, in a well-directed public unveiling at Watkins Glen in October. Time was getting short and back at Dearborn there were still a number of small problems to ease away by intensive application, an operation mercifully unchecked by doubts on the part of the man whose personality had forced through the project and whose future was riding on its

success. The car had a weight distribution problem, and a noisy exhaust that manifested itself as a humming sound around the 1800 rpm mark. But everyone who worked on the car was still in love with it, openly voicing their admiration and excitement with the product that had taken so much of their time, energy, skill and thought. As the release date neared, so the tension increased. One or two senior Ford managers predicted doom for the muscular little car, but Iacocca was never dissuaded or downhearted. As Gene Bordinat said of him, 'It took a lot of guts. He was putting his whole damn career on the line with that car.'

Communicating the message about a car may seem simple, but it requires discipline in thought and careful choice of words. Seeing a market among the young, among women drivers as well as macho sports car enthusiasts, Ford went into a huge publicity operation. Here the fact that there was a whole new market waiting to buy the car was turned to advantage. The thrust of the publicity was that of the beginning of a new era, and of Ford providing a new car for that new world. Up to that time, and this was only realized

later, the public had somehow equated small with cheap and big with expensive. The Mustang was to break this way of thinking for ever. Small could indeed be cheap, but the quality of luxury could still be there, and it was.

11,000 publications were mailed with the details, live stage presentations were put on in a dozen major cities for Ford Dealers, and a one-hour film on the car was shown in about 40 other cities. 200 of the nation's top radio presenters were offered test drives, and many were loaned a Mustang for a week.

But the biggest and best publicity opportunity was presented to the Mustang by a kindly Fate. This was the New York World's Fair to be held at Flushing Meadows, Queens. The Ford Pavilion had been created by Walt Disney and contained Ford's latest models, but instead of simply adding the Mustang to the list, Ford collected over 100 of the most important media people and gave them a preview of the Pavilion. The next day the media top brass were given a very special preview of the Mustang along with a crowd of 2000 media newsmen from Western Europe who had come to

preview the World's Fair for the press, radio and tv of the industrialized world.

After a presentation by Iacocca stressing the youth market's fun and style, and a promise of close involvement in competition driving, the new car was revealed. The media men were shown films, lunched and taken to witness the beginning of a 750-mile (1200-km) road rally. The press reported on the car's durability and reliability as a result of this well-organized rally, a major test for any new car. The media people also witnessed at first hand the spontaneous enthusiasm of the public, including sports car fans who drove up and challenged the Mustang drivers to race.

There followed on 16 April 1964, a unique media saturation event, on all three of the major tv networks. Between 9.30 and 10.00 pm the coverage reached 29,000,000 households. Thousands of newspapers, national magazines, all the auto publications, featured the new car. Iacocca and his four-wheel baby hit the front covers of *Time* and *Newsweek* simultaneously, a unique event in itself. Hundreds of millions of people were aware of the new car, and Iacocca just didn't leave it to Ford's advertising men. 'Whenever a writer or photographer came out here to work on a story about the car, he would drop whatever he was doing and spend a whole day, or sometimes two or three days, talking and answering questions. With a car like that, and with a guy like him pushing it, how could we miss?'

The result of all this is sometimes called 'Musclecar Madness' or, and much more accurately 'Mustang Mania.' It was a mania which, supported by a massive publicity campaign, was a measure of the excitement caused by the Mustang, for there was no denying that the car was very, very attractive.

At Huntsville, Alabama, a pre-release Mustang was used as a pace car and caused a massive scene of anarchy as 9000 spectators surged over walls and fences and surrounded the car, eager to see and touch this remarkable automobile. It took an hour before the authorities regained order and the race was then allowed to begin. On the release date of 17 April, public hysteria broke loose across the country as the showrooms were beseiged by thousands of people determined to own a Mustang, or else.

All available cars were sold immediately and dealers took orders for 22,000 in the first hours of opening. One said: 'I've never seen anything like it. People are in a trance when they come in. All they do is mutter, "I gotta have that car".' Some dealers had to lock their doors to avoid injury to life and limb; in one showroom 15 buyers began bidding with the dealer for the Mustang in his window, the last car and one which he was supposed to keep on display for at least a week. The dealer weakened as the bids went higher and higher and the lucky winner insisted on sleeping in the car all night until his cheque was cleared through the bank, just in case anyone else came in with a higher bid, or even cash. . . . He

A very rare version of the Mustang showcar with hard top.

was one of the lucky buyers, one individual among the 4,000,000 Americans who besieged Ford dealers in the first week of the Mustang release.

In over 300 public places across the land Mustangs were on display. Hundreds of draw winners were allowed use of a Mustang for a free week, the cars were in high demand to pace races, to transport beauty queens and other important people, and as prizes. Cars left parked in the street were covered with hand prints as crowds collected to touch and stroke the cars, as if they were a breed of exotic animal brought to civilization for the first time in history.

The Mustang soon sported the Industrial Designers' Institute Award and, a unique event for a car, was awarded the Tiffany Gold Medal Award. This highly-coveted award 'For Excellence in American Design' was presented to Henry Ford II by Walter Hoving, Tiffany's chairman, at the press introduction of the World's Fair.

Mustang Madness was not created by admen's superlatives; if anything, the ads showed as much style as the car by understatement. Once more it was Iacocca who gave the lead: 'Just put a big picture of the car up there so they can see how great it looks. . . . Then in big numbers let them see the price, $2368 f.o.b. Detroit. That's all you need to say.'

Of course there was body copy with options listed, but there was no danger here of creating clever lines to distract attention from the main attraction — car and price.

Even though the price was amazingly low for what was delivered as the base Mustang, it came as a surprise that only about 10 percent of Mustangs went at the lowest price. Most people wanted the V8 engine, and a selection of the options, making the average price more like $3000. It was in fact a specialist car with mass appeal, and none of the three faces of the Mustang seemed to clash with the other. There was the youthful economical face, the high-performance sports face and the luxury face of a mini-Thunderbird.

The problems of success began. When they ran out of V8 engines, Ford had to mount a special advertising campaign to attract young career women drivers to the six-cylinder model.

The press reaction had been enthusiastic, and in some quarters was ecstatic. *Car Life* said: 'It's a sports car, a gran turismo car, an economy car, a personal car, a rally car, a

This 64½ Mustang brought a breath of excitement to the suburbs.

sprint car, a race car, a suburban car, and even a luxury car.' *Car and Driver* said: 'Easily the best thing to come out of Dearborn since the 1932 V8 Model B roadster'.

Other stories claimed that the Mustang was on a par with foreign sports cars, even though it was a production car for the masses. The car's performance and styling were recommended by *Road and Track* and *Car Life*, which said: 'The car may well be, in fact, better than any mass-produced automobile on the basis of handling and roadability and performance, per dollar invested.'

There were, of course, some unflattering comments made of the first base Mustangs, especially driven at speed over tough conditions. This point, later answered by performance suspension, was countered by a few words of praise from that most difficult-to-please publication *Consumer Reports* which stated that the Mustang had 'almost complete absence of poor fit and sloppy workmanship in a car being built at a

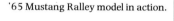

'65 Mustang Ralley model in action.

hell-for-leather pace.'

When motoring journalists eventually got their hands on the first HP car with its 271bhp 289 engine, heavy duty four-speed transmission, new suspension and Firestone Super Sport tires, the few doubts disappeared: 'Rear end stayed glued to the track no matter how hard we pushed it. Body lean was minimal. . . .' said *Motor Trend*.

It was inevitable that Mustang Madness would produce all manner of commercial spin-offs. Indeed Ford's first press ad offered a scale model of the new car for one dollar. The Mustang image and name appeared on all the expected T-shirts, sunglasses, hats, keychains and the rest. And while their parents were acquiring the real thing, 93,000 small children became proud owners of pedal-operated Mustang playcars.

Predictably the young owners of Mustang cars became dubbed the Mustang Generation, or simply 'Mustangers.' Mustang clubs, up to 400 of them eventually, were started by owners and aided by a special *Mustanger* magazine. These clubs, composed of enthusiastic Mustang owners who wanted to share the excitement of the car with each other, sponsored all manner of events such as gymkhanas, slaloms, autocrosses and hill climbs, for the pleasure of all ages, emphasizing that the Mustang was a family car as well as a sporty car capable of taking on the best of the competition from home and abroad. When Mustangs later began to make their impression on race events across the country these Mustang enthusiasts parked their cars in special 'Mustang Corrals.' These corrals, open to any Mustang that came along, were focal points for race supporters and also valuable contact areas between drivers and Ford officials.

What did Mustang Madness mean in sales terms? In six weeks the Mustang became the top-selling compact car, and ranked overall seventh in US car sales. In four months it had climbed to fifth place and by then more than 100,000 units had been sold. In the first 12 months of its life, the Mustang sold 418,812. This for a car that had first been grudgingly allowed a production rate of 75,000.

Sales people had predicted with gloom that if the car sold at all it would be at the expense of other Ford models, but this was not to be so. 50 percent of sales were won directly from the opposition.

Not only had the birth of Mustang been favored by the World's Fair, but the years 1964 and 1965 were set to be boom years. Things were so good that there were even income tax cuts! All this coincided with the coming-of-age of the wartime babies, with tremendous buying power suddenly at their disposal. Mustang was the right car at the right time. Iacocca modestly said, 'With all these ingredients it would have been hard not to succeed.' True, but the car had to be there and it had to be right. It *was* there, and it *was* right. That was not chance; it was the result of a lot of very hard work, a lot of commitment and a lot of leadership.

One very attractive part of the Mustang image, and it was to be financially a very profitable aspect for Ford, was the staggering number of available options, over fifty of them. The more important of these were air conditioning, four-speed manual transmission, three-speed automatic transmission, power brakes, power steering, racing or wire wheel covers, Rally Pac, radio, rear seat speaker, sports console, vinyl roof, rocker panel moldings, special suspension, outside rear view mirror, backing lights, padded sun shields, washers, compass, tachometer and exhaust cut-outs. Under the hood you could option the base Falcon engine with 170-cu in six, giving 101hp, or the 260-cu in Fairlane V8, delivering 160hp. Then there became available the 289-cu in V8 four-barrel, giving 210hp on regular fuel and, a few months after release, a mighty street version of the Shelby Cobra 289 which topped 271hp. This beast had 10.5:1 compression, solid lifters, strengthened train and dual exhausts. This powerful engine marked a new emphasis in the development of the Mustang, something that was to have wide-reaching consequences for the next successful year of the ponycar's life.

CHAPTER 5

MUSCLECAR MUSTANG

Previous page: '65 Mustang Fastback.
Air ducts were functional.

Views of a '65 convertible. Mustangs
became tougher, easier to ride and with
increased power.

The second-year Mustangs were generally beefed up. A few small changes were made and some more options came on stream, but the Mustang remained the Mustang and the three Ford plants thundered with activity to meet the huge demand.

The base engine became tougher, with 200-cu in displacement giving 120hp. The 260 V8 was phased out and replaced by a 289 two-barrel at 200hp.

New options included front disk brakes, a limited-slip differential, and steel wheels with styled design. Also available was a GT package, created to appeal to the racing driver inside everyone behind the steering wheel. This was to tie in with the GT 40 road racers carrying the Ford banner at home and abroad and consisted of dual exhausts, special-handling suspension, front disk brakes, fog lamps, a new instrument panel containing five gauges, GT identification and side stripes. This GT package was available for either of the four-barrel 289 engines.

But the smartest new thing around was the Mustang fastback 2-plus-2. It was launched on pure instinct. In May a secret clay model was unveiled to Iacocca. He had never seen it before and his reaction was in character. He is reported as saying, 'That's what I want. Go!'

The production 2-plus-2 fastback, which could have been called fast*buck* with equal truth, had a foldaway rear seat, functional air ducts in the rear pillar and attractive trim. It was to be the basis of a new track car called the Shelby GT 350.

The Mustang, though a powerful performer with its optional 289, was still in no trim to take on the GM opposition in the shape of Corvettes from Chevrolet or the majestic 389 GTO from Pontiac. Carrol Shelby, running a successful team of his own Cobras, was asked to take a look at the Mustang and give his advice on making it a true competitor of the GM cars on track. Shelby thought something could be done, though 100 production cars of the right specification had to be built to pass SCCA production car racer rules.

Shelby put together 12 2-plus-2 based racers by Christmas 1964 and one week later the Shelby team had, by some miracle of hard work, readied 100 racers for inspection by the SCCA. The car was declared legal for racing in small-block events. With help from a computer under the control of Klaus Arning of Ford, the suspension of the 2-plus-2 was tweaked to racing specifications. The new car was named the GT 350, mostly because it sounded a good name.

The GT 350 was a stripped-down 2-plus-2 to which was added a fiberglass hood with functional scoop, a racing steering wheel, competition seatbelts, tach and oil pressure gauge and special steel wheels.

The redesigned suspension incorporated Koni racing shocks, anti-hop axle torque arms, sway bar and tightened steering response. The brakes were front disk and rear drum with cooling for the race units. The output of the 289 was increased to 306hp using a high-rising aluminum manifold and four-barrel carb. Increased heat output was cooled by a bigger radiator and a $6\frac{1}{2}$-quart oil pan featuring internal baffles.

Of course the actual racing models had added custom refinements and some were reputed to reach almost 350hp. Additional axle race ratios were 3.70, 4.11 and 4.33.

Production of the GT 350 was a modest 562 in 1965, with 2378 units in 1966.

The new car dominated its class from the beginning and began winning a series of National Championships which continued into the coming years. Apart from the GT 350, Ford had a lot of racing going on. Mustangs won the '64 Tour de France, a Ford-engined Lotus driven by Jim Clark won the '65 Indianapolis 500, NASCAR circuits were dominated by Ford stock cars and Shelby's Cobras were defeating even the classic Ferraris in international competitions. There were now a few Ford Mark Is hitting the scene with Le Mans as the prize; these Mark Is had 7-liter engines. Joining this line-up of speed were the Mustang drag racers, mostly put together by enthusiasts but now with the beginnings of factory support.

As well as the practical Fords, there was also a series of Mustang-based show cars, one of which from Bertone of Turin won pride of place at the 1966 New York International

Auto Show. Although it is a good-looking car, this present writer at least is of the opinion that it was an unnecessary exercise; a pampered show car with a Continental accent might win prizes, but the home-grown Mustang was winning hearts.

September 1965 saw the unveiling of the 1966 Mustang. There was not a lot to unveil, which was a measure of the car's success. Inside, the GT instrument panel became standard on all cars and there were one or two added luxury options, such as a stereo tape deck and retracting seat belts.

The '66 changes on the Shelby GT 350 were the introduction of functional side scoops to cool the rear brakes, a less harsh suspension system, a muted exhaust and new plexiglass windshield. New GT 350 options came in under the hood. They were out of sight and included auto transmission, Detroit Locker rear axle and a Paxton supercharger that was reputed to surge the power way up above 400hp. New colors were made available and among these were the unique Hertz stable, in Hertz colors, that meant that anyone could 'Rent-a-Racer.'

1966 also saw the millionth Mustang come off the production line, on 23 February. The lucky owner of Mustang Number One traded it in for Mustang Number One-Million-and-One.

Some years earlier Iacocca had observed that people were prepared to pay anything for economy. His words were to echo through the accounting offices of Ford because, for some strange reason, nearly every Mustang sold took with it an average of $400-worth of options. This sent Ford's profits soaring to $1.1 *billion* dollars over the first two years of the Mustang's life.

Shelby GT 350 interior with Cobra logo.

Left: '65 Mustang interior with optional gauges and extras, designated Rally-Pac.

Opposite: '65 Shelby 350 with stripe in US racing colors.

Previous page: '65 adaptation of the Mustang was the Carrol Shelby Cobra. The hood scoop sucked air into a 289-cu in engine.

The '66 Mustang GT fastback carried the
289 engine developed for the Shelby
racing effort. Hertz had a herd of them so
that you could 'Rent a Racer'.

The '66 GT retained the central grille bar
but acquired many more practical
refinements. This model helped Mustang
break the half-million sales point with
panache.

'66 convertible with the redoubtable 289 engine.

CHAPTER 6

SON OF MUSTANG

The '67 Mustang was to be the second generation, whose gestation period started as soon as the first Mustang began turning heads on the streets.

The problems were in a sense made more complex by success. Would the success last? Should the new model be along the same lines, or should it show definite development? And what was the opposition up to? How would a second-generation Mustang show up when the competition arrived, as it was bound to?

The man in charge of the '67 was Hal Sperlich, who was of the opinion that the new Mustang should be better in every respect than the original. There should be more models, more options, better handling, better performance, keener braking, greater comfort, more efficiency and a smoother, quieter ride. But, even so, how far should the actual appearance be changed?

As far as the engineering went, it was admitted there was room for improvement. The Mustang had come together in a hurry, it was a winner, but it had not received the ultimate attention it had deserved. The '67 project was a chance to tighten up all round. Specifically, this meant paying attention to the ride and handling, with fine adjustments to the '66 Falcon/Fairlane chassis components over original '64 Falcon items, adjustments to the shape of the car's forward regions to accommodate the proposed new big-block 390-cu in V8 engine and a new power unit to give Mustang performance to challenge the hairier Pontiac GTO threat. All this was tangible nuts-and-bolts stuff which simply required high levels of input.

The design job was something else. The brief was 'Change it, but don't change it.' To this end, the basic Mustang shape was evolved and pulled and pushed and pinched and streamlined in half a dozen new conceptual directions, which went to every possible point on the styling compass. In fact they were trying to improve the Mustang without destroying the identity or losing the family resemblance to the $1\frac{1}{2}$ million Mustangs out there on the roads. This design project was started before the phenomenal success of the Mustang became fully realized. They tried everything, producing cars of every possible variation on the theme. Some were so varied that they were different cars completely, which was the wrong direction. Certain cues were set — the front end for example — and the Mustang proportions of $\frac{1}{3}:\frac{2}{3}$ regarding the silhouette.

The answer came after a lot of hard work and blind alleys and was in fact a strengthening of the original Mustang theme. It was a design that was broader, wider, deeper-sculpted and more solid. It was slightly more bulged to take the extra power, but the bulge was all muscle; there was no fat on this new design. In fact the shape sang out 'performance' while being impossible to mistake for anything else but Mustang.

Mustang Mania was still in full swing, maybe not so wild but certainly deeper. The car was firmly lodged in the national consciousness, especially in the younger part of that consciousness. It would have been counterproductive at this stage to have evolved the car too rapidly away from its original shape.

Under the new skin, changed but not changed, the engineering was tightened up, making for a firmer ride. With the added power of the new engine there was great concern that the handling should be safe. With this in mind, many of the refinements developed by Shelby for the racers were not taken advantage of, for Ford was aware that the street Mustangs would be driven by ordinary citizens who might have found the fine responses of the Shelby system dangerous in some situations.

Now that the Mustang had to carry a big 390-cu in V8, there was a lot of redesigning to do regarding weight distribution. The car was in danger of becoming nose-heavy, something that had already happened and was to happen again with other high-performance autos. The Mustang acquired a very large stabilizer bar in front and adjustments in rear to compensate for the heavier nose. The result was successful, for the new set-up gave lots of lower-end torque, was no slouch down the straight and was safe in cornering.

One of the very few negative comments about the original Mustang was a lack of leg room, so the design group moved the rear seat back as much as they could, allowing a little relief in the front for long-limbed drivers.

The resulting '67 Mustang was generally considered to be a true Mustang, plus. The car had grown a few inches in each direction, with half an inch extra overhead, track at 58 inches front and rear, width nearly three inches more and length two inches plus, and the weight was increased by 140 lbs. The grille was larger, the side sculptures deeper, there was a special hood with two indentations for engine vents and turn-signals and the rear panel was concave. There were wide-oval sports tires and also quad exhaust tips for the GT models.

The instrument panel had a five-gauge set, two large and three small, and the panel extended across the width of the car, joining an upward-swept center console integrating the T-shaped gear shift lever. Optional instruments could be added to this padded arrangement, giving the driver parking brake lights, door ajar lights, fuel demand light and seat belt reminder lights.

The Mustang buyer now had a choice of five power units: 200-cu in Six, 289 V8 Challenger (200hp), 289 V8 Challenger Special (225hp), 289 Cobra (271hp), and of course the big 390 V8 Thunderbird Special (320hp). Transmissions included three-speed floor shift with full synchronization, four-speed close ratio manual and, for the first time, a combined automatic-manual named the Select-shift Cruise-O-Matic. This was the first Ford automatic that also allowed manual shift. The designation for these cars was GT-A.

Steering was made safer and more precise with newly developed ball-joint sockets filled with polyethylene, reducing the turning circle diameter by five feet.

Federal regulations brought in new safety items and Ford added others on their own initiative. These included dual hydraulic braking, brake fail-safe light, padding on armrests, pillars, visors and panels, safety handles on doors, seat belt reminder lights, emergency flashers, shatterproof glass and corrosion-resistant brake linings.

The popularity of the Mustang grew as its sales figures climbed. The car was rated readers' favorite for the third year in succession in a poll conducted by Car and Driver magazine. By the end of March 1967, Ford had sold Mustangs to the retail value of nearly $5 billion, and the average option addition to base sales prices had risen to $500 per unit. People were spending more than they strictly needed to, because they were devoted to the Mustang ponycar concept.

Previous page: '67 Shelby Mustang GT 500 — the greediest car on the road.

The '67 GT fastback had increased power and more grille area. The front sculpture was deeper, giving the car a longer-nosed look.

Left: While retaining its Mustang identity, the '67 Mustang put on visible muscle, became wider and more streamlined. It was voted 'Outstanding Car of the Year' by the readers of *Car & Driver.*

Below: '67 Mustangs entered the Trans Am series with the Shelby team and ace driver Jerry Titus.

The '67 Shelby 500.

Mid-year production figures for 1967 were 472,121, despite an acknowledged slow-down in total industry sales.

Changes for 1968 were few, mostly to meet new safety regulations and Phase One emission-control rules. There was now a collapsible steering column, new lights and redesigned internal features such as knobs and handles.

The engine line-up was as follows:

200 cu in Six 115hp
289 cu in V8 195hp
302 cu in V8 230hp
390 cu in V8 325hp
427 cu in V8 390hp

Above these was the sculptured hood which now became standard with its built-in vents and turn signals. New options included rear window defogger, collapsible spare tire and a special package of Sports Trims which included two-tone hood, woodgrain panel, styled wheels and wide-oval tires for V8s. New radial tires were also available in small numbers, the first signs of a coming tire revolution.

The Shelby cars became more and more Ford and less and less Shelby. Shelby himself was deep into racing efforts, and production was moved from the Shelby factory on the West Coast to Michigan. There were a few changes to styling, longer hood scoops, new tail lamps and new front lights. New emission standards meant a decrease in engine power and the GT350 now had a 302-cu in engine giving 250hp. A new impact was made, however, by a convertible model with integral padded roll-bar. Loss of power did not hurt the sales

Shelby's GT 500 Mustang put lessons learned on the racetrack back into the design studios and engineering workshops, where they helped to mold the look and the performance of the production Mustangs.

The 'Cobra' logo reminds us that the very first Mustang had AC Cobra associations.

The coiled power of the Cobra-Jet engine.

of Shelby cars, which reached a new high of 4450 for 1968.

Also new was the fastback Mustang E with extra large torque, converter automatic and 2.33:1 rear axle, powered by a new 250-cu in Six giving 155hp. In addition there was the 390 V8 twin-barrel carb at 280hp. The hardtop optioned a trim package, identified as GT/SC or GT/Sports Coupé consisting of fog lamps, exposed hood latches, side stripes, scoop, rear spoiler and Cougar-Shelby rear lights.

But most thrilling of all was the Ford 428 Cobra-Jet engine, which made its debut mid-year. It had a vacuum-activated ram-air hood scoop, flat-black mid-hood area and side stripes identifying its GT nature — as if anyone could miss it! The Cobra-Jet produced 335 horsepower at 5400 rpm and the torque hit 440 lb-ft at 3400 rpm. With a compression ratio of 10.6:1 went high performance 427 cylinder heads, a 735 CFM Holley four-barrel carb and wide-open air intakes and exhausts from header-type exhaust manifolds. Transmission was either four-speed or automatic to 3.50:1 or 3.91:1 or 4.30:1 rear axle. Tires were Goodyear Polyglas wide-ovals and the whole Cobra-Jet deal was available on all three Mustang styles. The engine won a higher classification for NHRA competitions, with the Cobra-Jet equipped Mustang in drag trim doing the quarter-mile in under 12 seconds.

In road racing, the first two Trans Am series in '66 and '67 were taken by the Mustang. The new race was soon to become the classic US series and in the first two years Shelby and Ford's race manager, Jacques Passino, put together a formidable team behind the formidable Mustang.

TOTAL PERFORMANCE

'Spare Time'

One thing the automotive industry can never do is to stand still. With two, and more often three, years needed to take a new model from first sketches to production, with the competition breathing hard down your neck all the time, with new materials and fashions to be taken into account, with new Federal regulations and standards to be complied with, the life of the car maker is not exactly of tranquil ease.

Even before the '67 Mustang was in production the first '69 designs, based on the '65 car, were being considered and discussed. The main difference was in the headlight area and the design played a new tune on the side-scoop theme, an alternative being to lose it altogether and replace it with two groups of horizontal louvers stacked up just fore of the rear wheels. One thought was to bring the nose well forward of the headlamps, another to bring up the whole front to a smooth curve with hidden lights. Both ideas were obviously Mustang and both were pleasing in their own way. As thinking developed, the nose grew longer and lower, the side-scoops disappeared and a front fender line reached all the way back and swooped up to the roof behind the door. This design was too far from Mustang and, though a good-looking beast, had no identity. Some other ideas were ahead of their time, and dynamic in both the targa-topped example and an ultra fastback whose long low-diving roof made it look like a station wagon — but what a station wagon! This design made it as far as a glass-fiber construction. It was beautiful, but too far from the Mustang identity.

In the search for identity, clay models were made, using the Mustang cues and incorporating ideas that were later to appear in the final '69 design. There was a softly-rounded theme, a theme with pronounced air-outlet ducts, one with rectangular lights and forward scoops, another with distinctive window and roof lines.

There was of course a strong influence from the Thunderbird, three-element tail lights featuring strongly together with rear-facing scoops. The designers also tried making the Mustang shorter, but had to put back the lost length for stowage and fuel facilities.

Final decisions had to be made. It turned out, happily, that the proposed changes did not stray too far from the Mustang image that was still turning people on to the concept of the small, performance car.

The hidden-headlamp theme was abandoned in favor of a quad group, two in and two out of the grille, the roof line developed a built-in spoiler and was designated 'Sports Roof,' parking lights went under the fender, the six rear lamps in sets of three were brought away from the surface of the rear panel and on the 2-plus-2 the sail panel louvers were abandoned in favor of quarter windows. The coupés and convertibles had outlet trims in front of the rear wheels and non-functional scoops adorned the Sports Roof model.

The main objective had been to tweak the performance of the previous model and make the optional V8 better.

The 1969 optional V8 derived from the '68 390 and rated 428. It came, and went, in two versions which although seemingly rated the same did in fact have crucial differences. They were the 428 V8 and the 428 Cobra-Jet Ram-Air V8.

The Cobra-Jet Ram-Air V8 had a 737 c.f.m. 4-bbl and its internal components were of drag engine durability. Its

The '68 Shelby GT 500 models had forward-moved hoodscoop (compare with the picture on page 40). Lucas foglamps replace the previous central hi-beams. Though his name was up there on the front, Shelby's influence was in decline and the '68 Shelby-Mustangs were built in Michigan.

advertised power and torque were in fact wildly underrated, for it was a drag engine playing peekaboo with the drag authorities and insurance companies.

A two-years-old show car, the Mach 1, a two-seater with big rear scoops and ducktail fastback, was brought out, dusted over and shown again as a teaser for the '69 car. In the days before the emissions and safety lobbies grew strong, and before oil crises hit the Western world, the emphasis on heavy performance was unashamed.

Early in '68 Ford had headhunted Bunkie Knudson from GM to become the new Ford Company President, having just missed the Presidential desk at GM. There was nothing he could do to change the '69 program but he entered Ford like a hairy, growling dragster and was soon burning rubber down the executive corridor.

He marshalled the Ford battalions to create a killer car that would blow his former employers' products into the weeds, and the main target was the Camaro Z28. Knudsen wanted to turn the Mustang into the nearest thing to a Trans Am racer on the road, within the limits of financial possibility. The main problem with the Mustang was handling. Knudsen wanted to make it the best handling car on the market and he would not be satisfied with second place. Of course they wanted to call it Trans Am, but Pontiac had got there first (an interesting side note being that GM had wanted to use the Mustang name, but were squeezed out by Ford in '64). The new Mustang package was to be known as BOSS 302, named for the 302 V8 super-muscled derivative of Ford's racing engine.

Matt Donner, leader of the ride and handling group, found

the Boss 302 so fast that he insisted on wearing SCCA regulation helmet and fireproof racing overalls when driving the prototypes on the Dearborn test track.

There were problems. When they added huge, hard F60 tires and put the car through the rough road programme, the rocky tires, in the words of Ford engineer Howard Freers, '. . . literally tore up the front end of the car. The upper control arm mounts bolted through the front suspension tower structure, and that tire was so rough it was breaking the towers.'

To cure this problem they had to add considerable reinforcements which had to be on all models.

All these delights were to come. The '69 made its debut with two new choices, the Mach 1 and a luxury hardtop named Grandé. The Mach 1 had as standard a 351-cu in engine giving 250hp and an optional 428, new suspension, exposed hood locks, woodgrain console, dual racing mirrors and stripes. Grandé, aimed at the luxury end of the market, had a teakwood look throughout, cloth and vinyl seats, wire wheelcovers, soft rear suspension and increased sound insulation. On all models the central pillar was moved forward by four inches to allow better access to the rear seats and there was increased internal ventilation.

Under the hood of the '69 series there was a choice of 200-cu in Six, 250-cu in Six, 302 V8, two 351 V8 models, a 390 V8, a regular 428 and the Cobra-Jet Ram-Air 428. Innovative options included a three-spoke racing style wheel, power ventilation that fed cool air through the car when parked and a Traction-Lok which limited slip differential.

The Shelby GTs became more and more customized

Far left: The '67–69 Mustang Mach II prototype had mid-engine design.

Left: This view of the '67 Mustang production model shows the sunroof option and the way in which the nose had begun to point forward.

Below: The '67 Mustang fastback shows how the rear molding had begun to assume a ducktail shape, an embryonic spoiler.

products but their front grille and flat nose were a preview of future Mustangs. Other parts were unique, like the five NACA scoops on the hood and four other functional scoops. New Shelbys had luxurious upholstery and a new 351 Windsor unit 290hp with finned aluminum valve covers. The Shelby 428 cu in GT 500 remained unaltered.

In September a group of drivers and three special Mach 1 Mustangs gathered at Bonneville Salt Flats to try grabbing some speed and endurance records. They were wildly successful, scoring 295 United States Auto Club records. In one 24-hour long distance run they averaged an incredible 157 mph.

Ford was setting records of all kinds, and winning races on road tracks, race tracks and drag strips. But it had yet to make its mark on the performance-oriented production market, despite its successful Mustang sales. Bunkie Knudsen was to change all that with the Cobra-Jet package and his ex-GM muscle philosophy. He found he had a lot of people eager to get power into the Mustang. Like Jacques Passino, the race boss, who said, 'I think if we give the kids the power,

'68 Mustang GT. Side stripe emphasises the traditional Mustang recessed panel.

'68 Shelby 500 version of the Mustang.

they'll buy the tires and clip the springs and do whatever else they have to do to get the traction. But, first they need the power.' Passino had already done this with the 428 for the Trans Am and stock races. Knudsen now gave Roy Lunn of Kar Kraft the task of getting the massive 429 high-performance engine into the Mustang production model in order to qualify the set-up. The job had to be done and 500 minimum production cars had to be built. They squeezed in that engine until the car was at bursting point, and the result was the BOSS 429. It was underrated at 375hp, had massive components and reworked handling and suspension. It featured aluminum heads with canted valves, semi-combustion chambers, forged steel crankshaft, connecting rods, pistons and rocker arms, hi-rise aluminum intake manifold, dry decking, front spoiler and huge hood scoops for the ram-air system. It also had seven-inch-wide chrome rims, Goodyear Polyglas tires, front and rear sway bars, staggered rear shocks, and super-stiff springs. Despite the added load, the distribution of the vehicle's weight was 56 percent front and 44 percent rear. The four-speed and 3.91:1 locking rear

This page shows views of activity at Bonneville around the '69 Mustang Mach 1. The aggressive-looking grille had begun to give the car a deeply sculptured feel, hardly softened by the glassed-in lights.

Opposite page : The '69 Shelby GT 350 had unusual triple scoops and a mouth that enclosed lights and grille.

Overleaf: Bonneville is the backdrop for Mickey Thompson's '69 Mustang. The recessed panel has gone and the rear fender lacks scoop, which most Cobras possessed.

axle drove the wheels, which had power steering and manual disk brakes. There were to be no luxuries, only performance goodies. The idea was to remain competitive in stock racing and 1375 were built, to the everlasting delight of the car connoisseur. Roy Lunn also produced a mid-engine model with the 429 driving a conventional rear axle, saving the costs involved in designing a new style transaxle.

The specialist press acclaimed the new models. The Mach 1 was named 'the best Mustang yet and quickest ever' (*Car Life*, February 1979). It went on to say, 'By choosing the optimum combination of suspension geometry, shock absorber valving and spring rates, Ford engineers have exempted the Mach 1 from the laws of momentum and inertia, up to unspeakable speeds.'

The speeds were in fact measurable. Acceleration 0–60 was clocked at 5.5 seconds and the quarter-mile was done in 13.9 seconds. The test car concerned gave a speed of 121 mph at 6000 rpm in fourth gear.

The advent of the BOSS 302 small-block could not be missed by anyone as the only colors available were bright yellow, Wimbledon white, Calypso Red and Acapulco Blue. Having had their eyes fried by these colors, the enthusiasts were then treated to a treasure chest of engineering when they opened the hood.

First of all, two versions of the engine, one for street and one for track. The street engine was capable of delivering 290hp at 5800 rpm; torque was 290 ft/lbs at 4300 rpm. The racing engine was capable of 450 horsepower. Canted valve

cylinder heads sucked air through a high-rise intake manifold and the street engine carb was a 780 c.f.m. Holley four-barrel.

Canting the valves meant a triangular chamber, speedier in-and-out flow cylinder-wise, greater pushrod clearance, more room for bigger valves, 2.33-inch intakes and 1.7-inch exhausts. Solid valve lifters meant a quicker cam and more precise valve timing, resulting of course in a faster operation all round. All relevant components were massive, forged steel brutes capable of giving and taking the merciless pounding of rods and pistons. Forged crankshafts were electronically balanced for statics and dynamics while running. Rocker covers were chromed or cast-aluminum, there was a high capacity dual-point ignition system, four-speed manual transmission and a 3.5:1 rear axle. Optional axles were 3.91:1 and 4.30:1.

The engine was of course the main attraction. It gave the car a 56/44 front-to-rear weight distribution. Naturally, the suspension had to be heavy duty and used the staggered shock arrangement. Steering had a 16:1 ratio, and quick response resulted from the lock-to-lock movement of only 3.71 turns of the steering wheel. The strengthened body had wider wheel openings to allow space for the F60-15 fiber-glass-belted tires; wheels were seven-inch wide magnum styled steel or optional magnum 500 steel wheels which were chromed. Tread width increased to 59½ inches front and rear. To control this heavy package, Ford supplied floating-caliper front disk brakes, the disks being of ventilated cast iron.

Opposite page: Shelby GT 500 with scoops all over.

'69 Supercharged Shelby.

Below: Supercharged Shelby showing front spoiler. The fastest snow plow?

The race-intended version of the engine had allowance for dry decking instead of the usual gaskets, special intake manifold made up of individual channels, two four-barrel Holleys, each feeding 1100 c.f.m. to its own cylinder, and tuned tubular exhaust headers. To prevent oil surge around tough corners the cast-aluminum pan had a windage tray while the race-style crankshaft acquired better high-rev lubrication by being cross-drilled. Other differences between the race model and the street model were forged steel valves with hollow stems and tulip heads and sodium-filled exhaust valves which meant quicker cooling. Work and experience on the GT 40 Le Mans victor supplied the heavier connecting rods and bolts.

What did the press think?

'Without a doubt the Boss 302 is the best handling Ford ever to come out of Dearborn and may just be the new standard by which everything from Detroit must be judged . . . a hell of an enthusiast's car. It's what the Shelby GT350s and 500s should have been . . .' (Car and Driver, June '69).

'On the street the Boss 302 is more flexible (than the Z28) . . . easier to drive in a casual manner . . . much more power off the line, and with its bigger tires it had more traction' (Car Life, September '69).

Despite a real effort, the Mustang was unable to win the Trans Am series that year, being foiled by Camaro. The series had attracted a lot of attention from other manufacturers, who were taking the ponycar image as seriously as Ford. The battle on the tracks was a foretaste of the battle soon to be waged in showroom and street as Chevrolet, Pontiac and American Motors went after the profitable musclecar market that the Mustang had opened up.

For 1970 Bunkie Knudsen had ordered the removal of the non-functional side scoops from all models. This scoop was the

last vestige of the strong side panel sculpturing that had been one of the instant recognition cues of the original Mustang. In September '69 the 1970 Mustangs were introduced, minus side scoops. A week later Henry Ford ordered the removal of Bunkie Knudsen himself. Knudsen was not fired just because he scrubbed the side scoops. There were many other reasons to do with personality clashes, management style, and all the other human relations factors. Knudsen had created the magnificent Boss 302, but maybe his tire marks had scorched too many Ford toes. . . . All that can be said with certainty is that there was a definite smell of burning rubber in the corridors of power. Knudsen came and went like a fire-breathing drag racer.

To get back to the 1970 Mustangs, they were not much different from the '69 cars. The grille opening was a little wider, the rearquarter panels slightly smoother. Tail lamps were recessed into the rear panel and there were stripes and such, mostly cosmetic changes to the outside. Standard tires were now fiberglass-belted and standard seating was the high-back bucket seat taken from the Mach 1 '69 model. Four-speed cars had a new Hurst shifter and linkage, there were semi-oval steering wheels with either two or three spokes, externally adjustable headlamps and a non-reversing odometer. New options included automatic seatback releases, reflective side-marker safety lamps duplicating turn signals, new safety belts for passengers and transmission/steering/ignition safety locks. Sports Roof Mustangs could now option the Boss-style rear window louvers and adjustable rear spoiler.

There was a new engine option, too, a big-block 351-cu in four-barrel V8 using the canted valve system, as in the 429. The other engines were given improvements but were not much changed otherwise.

Previous page: The mighty Boss 302, with details of its muscle. This 1970 powerhouse was the Mach I, and then plus some.

The modified light arrangement on the Boss 302 helped soften the front.

The rear louvers and spoiler on the '70 Boss 302 failed to lighten an ungainly part of the car (*below*).

A '70 hoodscooped Boss sits between (right) the '70 Shelby and (left) a 1965 Shelby Cobra.

Bottom right: Standard Mustang '70. The new horizontal-bar grille with floating emblem helped achieve a cleaner front end, but the car was overgrown.

'70 Boss 302 Mustang. Its 302 V8 derived from the small-block Ford engine and it was fielded as a challenge to Chevy's Camaro Z-28.

Right: Side view of the Boss 302 shows the pointy nose that came to be called the 'Bunkie beak'. Early trials with hard tires caused problems with the suspension, requiring structural reinforcements to the chassis.

A prototype car, called the Quarter Horse, was built. It was a proposed replacement for both the Shelby and the Boss 429 and combined Shelby front-end body work, the 429 engine, and the Mercury Cougar instrument panel. The idea was to make it cheaper to build than a GT500, with better looks than the Boss 429 and more power and performance than the Mach 1 428. It did away with the Shelby scoops and had the Sports Roof with duck-tail spoiler as an integral part. It did not get into production.

Ford was still racing and was to have the success it craved in the '70 Trans Am series. Bud Moore led the team which enjoyed massive Ford funding and factory back-up. The series was hotly contested by Ford, Chevy, Pontiac, Plymouth, Dodge and AM. Parnelli Jones scored five wins for Mustang and George Follmer scored one to bring Ford overall victory. AM Javelins driven by Penske and Donohue, despite entering the series late, scored three firsts to secure second overall placing.

Some of the success must have been due to a new 'Cross-Boss' intake manifold to provide greatly enhanced mid-range power.

The 1970 Trans Am series is considered to have been the high point in the series' history as regards the number of marques and intensity of factory input. Future Mustangs would be heavier and the Trans Am series would from now on be depleted in terms of events and variety of competition.

Colorful paintwork on the Boss 302 was an attempt to swing with the times. Journalists ignored the cosmetics and declared that the car was 'the best handling Ford ever to come out of Dearborn'.

The colorful beast about to hit the quarter-mile.

Manufacturers were pulling out fast and turning their resources towards meeting the heavy commitment of Federal requirements regarding emission controls, safety standards and durability of construction.

To sign off this chapter, and indeed the Trans Am series itself, here are the results *Road and Track* magazine recorded on George Follmer's racing Mustang: 0–60 in 5.5 seconds, quarter-mile in 12.9 sec at 110 mph, top speed 151 mph at 7500 rpm in fourth gear. A dark cloud passed over Detroit, stopped and refused to move on. It threw its shadow into every corporate boardroom, office, design studio and engineering workshop. The message was clear. No more power cars, no more performance, no more fun driving. The dark cloud was composed of a mass of rules and regulations that effectively strangled any glints of 'performance.' The word itself, which used to mean power, began to be used in a different way; it took on an economy tinge.

DARK DAYS

Unfortunately the Mustang's shape and characteristics had been set down in the short Knudsen era and they were size, weight and high horsepower. No account had been taken of the new limitations put on engines regarding emissions and safety. Little flexibility was possible to allay the fears of the safety lobbies and the sharp eyes of the insurance companies.

The Mustang's real problem was that it had begun to lean too far into the luxury market. Naturally the accountants wanted to make what profits were available in this sector, so management decreed bigger cars, quieter cars, easier riding cars, cars with bigger engines. The Mustang had begun to swell and the original concept of a small, sporty car that could zip along in a stylish manner was in real danger of being lost. The planners were trying to make it all things to all people. Planners have always wanted that, a universal-selling model they can manufacture cheaply. Nobody has ever got there yet and nobody is ever likely to. So the Mustang got bigger and heavier, but suddenly people wanted economy, safety and lower emission levels.

The first clay models for 1971 were monstrous great things, hugely ugly, bulgingly fat. They were soon slimmed down, slimmed down again, and a few of their more creative aspects retained. A reasonable-looking but still large car was the result, with pleasing side creases. But a sedan look was beginning to creep into the picture. More work was needed. Early in '68 the '71 design was nearly set. A long and low fastback with fender scoops, its grille and lights were deeply recessed and the rear lights were high in the ducktail end. Bunkie Knudsen saw it in the studio and said 'Yes' immediately. Chief designer Gail Halderman asked if he wanted to see it outside. No, he didn't; this was it. 'We never had approvals like that before,' mused Halderman. In fact Knudsen was to remove all non-functional scoops before final production.

It was the task of chief engineer Howard Freers to work out the handling and drivelines of the '71, and as new regulations were passed their implications had to be taken into account. The Boss 302 engine was wonderful, but also wonderfully expensive. They decided to replace it with a cheaper 351. The 428s were also replaced, by three versions of the 429 V8, the Cobra-Jet, the Cobra-Jet Ram-Air and the Super Cobra-Jet. With canted valve heads making the new engine bigger, the car had to be fattened-up to $61\frac{1}{2}$ inches tread-width in front and 60 inches in the rear.

One of the new safety regulations, a side guard door beam, was put to unexpected test on a road trip, when another motorist crossed a red light and smashed into a '71 prototype worth $150,000. The guard beam worked.

A preview of the '71 arrived in the shape of a car (strictly for show) called the Mustang Milano, a slim and slinky two-seater with split grille and concealed headlights. Painted in violet, it attracted a lot of attention and prepared people's expectations for the '71 series.

This series represented the greatest change in the Mustang shape ever, and there was a great deal of doubt about the direction in which the Mustang was going, especially among those who had been responsible for the original car. Lee Iacocca publicly stated that the Mustang had been removed from its original class because of the way the Boss 429 had been shoehorned into it, distorting it out of all recognition. The evil cause, in his words, was '. . . performance, performance, performance!' He may have realized that the words *performance* and *Knudsen* were very closely allied. . . .

There was no lack of luxurious style; the Sports Roof model was dramatic, the Mach 1 was mach-o and the Boss bossy. But were they still ponycars? Or were they heavy cavalry mounts?

Well, as one Ford employee said of the '71 car: 'It was Bunkie's Mustang, the one that looked like it hit the wall.'

This wall-hitter was 600 pounds heavier and had a large number of new options and features. Flush door-handles outside, concealed windshield wipers, large speedo, tach, oil, alternator and temperature gauges, radio, heater, clock, pull-type inner door-handles, longer arm rests; a miniconsole with gear lever and ashtray came as standard.

Left: '71 Mustang convertible with new grille and front end.

Far left: Cobra Jet engine 351.

1971 Boss 351. Good-looking, but too big.

Previous page: '71 Mustang Mach I.

The base engine was now the 250-cu in Six and there were up to six separate optional V8 engines. Lower-powered Mach 1 had a two-barrel 302 with optional two- or four-barrel 351 or a 429 cu in giving 370hp, with a further option of the Ram-Air system. Additional 3.90:1 or 4.11:1 rear axle options could beef it up further if wanted. The Boss 351 had the new high-performance 351 High Output (Cleveland) rated at 330hp.

Steering gear was redesigned to constant ratio with the standard suspension, with a variable ratio available with the competition class chassis. The Mach 1 had a urethane front bumper in body color and the Boss 351 had its aerodynamic chin spoiler. Options included power windows, rear glass defroster and a vinyl cover for the Sports Roof.

We've already seen how the major new safety addition, side guard beams, had been proved on the road accidentally, but there were also emissions regulations to comply with. These requirements were answered by an air injection system, IMCO or Improved Combustion, fitted to all models except the Boss 351 and Drag-Packed 429s, where thermal reactors were installed to cut down on hydrocarbons and carbon monoxide. An evaporative emission system was also required and in California, where the rules were more stringent, cars had to be fitted with exhaust gas recirculation (EGR) in order to control Nitrogen Oxides (NOx) which were rightly considered to be noxious.

Withdrawal of excessive warranties saved Ford money, in line with the other major companies who were also dropping long-time long-mileage warranties. Unfortunately, all prices were increased.

Right: 1972 Mustang Mach I.

Below right: The overgrown '71 Boss 351 called 'Bunkie's Mustang' was to be axed after prolonged battles inside the corridors of power.

1972 Mustang in drag racing trim. The Mustang somewhere under the rebuilding is one of the last of the overgrown ponies. Smaller cars were soon to return.

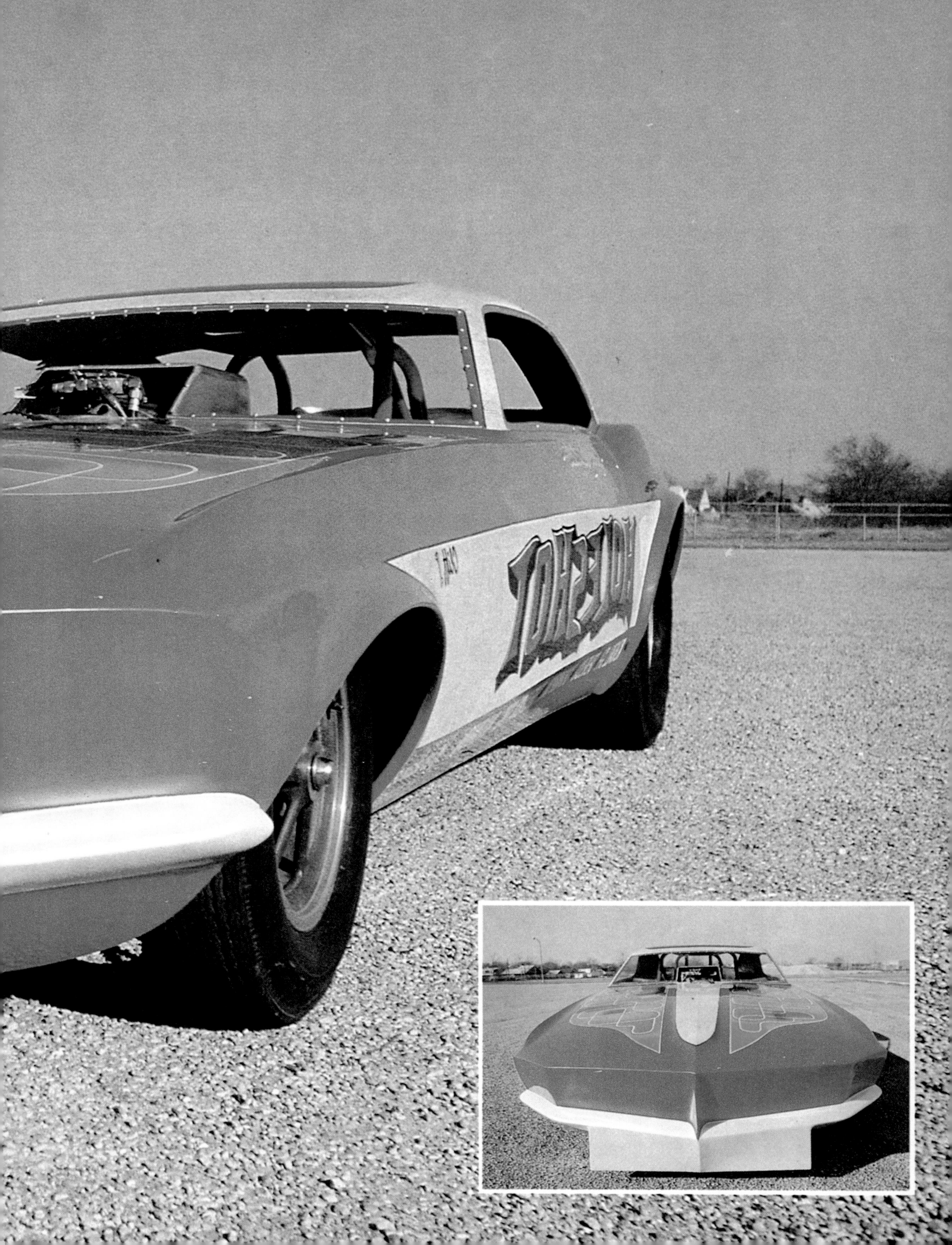

Many claims were made for the new Boss 351 in the handling and tractability sections. It came with stronger springs and sway bars, four-speed transmission with T-handle shift and Hurst linkage. In fact there were two Boss 351 power units: 351-4V with compression ratio of 10.7:1, giving 285hp at 5400 rpm and 351-4V HO, compression ratio 11.7:1, giving 330hp at 5400 rpm. Both had torque of 370 ft/lb at 3400 and 4000 rpm respectively. The Sports Roof was nearly horizontal and this produced some visibility defects, but the motoring press thought it an advance over the previous rear slats and spoiler.

Forbidden to go all out for performance, some Ford executives made the error of trying to give lower-priced cars a 'performance' feel by decking them out in the cosmetics of custom cars, with stripes, scoops and black-out trim. This warpaint did not make heroes out of rookies and probably damaged the image of the Mustang. The real problem was that sales were falling; for the model year '71 they hit a record low of 139,942.

Ford was in some kind of paradox. It had a new big car that was underpowered for its image and in 1972 had to drop all claims of performance. There were five '72 models: Standard hardtop, Grandé hardtop, standard Sports Roof, Mach 1 Sports Roof and the convertible. There were five engines all running on low octane gas: 250-cu in, 302-2V V8, 351-2V V8, 351-4V V8 and 351-4V HO. It is painfully significant that Ford thought it best not to publish any output figures and instead made claims about the effectiveness of its emissions controls. This must have been the darkest shadow from that dark cloud hovering over Detroit. The Federal authorities tried to create a little light by lifting excise tax on passenger cars. Combined with a cut in dealer percentage, this resulted in a lowering of the price by $150.

In the darkness, battles had been raging at Dearborn over the weakened but still reasonably powerful performance of the 351 HO. Top brass were frightened of bringing out anything that even hinted at 'performance,' while the engineers knew that there were still buyers for muscular cars. Only about a thousand were built, after a lot of trouble.

There was also a new SAE rating system, a nett system which measured performance, while the engine was actually interfaced with all it had to drive, rather than being rated on a test bench. SAE rating figures were nett rather than gross, but even so the 351 HO produced a creditable performance: 0–60 in 6.6 seconds, quarter-mile in 15.1 sec at 95.6 mph and a top speed of 120 mph.

In February the Mustang's image was severely damaged when the public were offered a Sprint Decor Option. Truly described as a dumb gimmick, it attempted to dress up the Mustang without delivering the performance, but the unkindest thing was that the same option was also available for the Pinto and Maverick cars. If Ford themselves didn't have faith in the Mustang as something special and had begun to treat it as a cheapo thrill, then who wanted a Mustang? Mustang sales ground down to a miserable 119,920 (remind yourself that nearly 420,000 Mustangs were sold in its first year). It was small consolation that Mustang's competitors were doing even worse. A tiny spot of light fell on Dearborn in March '72 when *Popular Hot Rodding* magazine voted the Mustang 'Car of the Decade.' Fine, but where were the buyers?

The new, fat, underpowered Mustang was little changed for 1973. A new grille with vertical parking lamps appeared, there was a dab of paint here and there, all standard bumpers, now urethane, protruded a little way out and were linked to shock-absorbing items in the structure. The EGR system was developed to control emissions while retaining drivability, there were power front brakes as standard on convertibles and 351 V8s, and longer shock absorbers. Options included forged aluminum wheels, steel-belted radial tires, leather-wrapped steering wheel and non-functional scoops on the two-tone hood. The best that could be said was that it still did look a classy performance-promising auto. All ponycar manufacturers were taking a close look at their products. The Barracuda, the Challenger and the Javelin were to be dropped, and GM only saved its Camaro and Firebird after prolonged and fierce internal argument.

The future did not look all that bright.

1973 Mustangs like this one were still bulky and overdressed. There is hardly space for anything else in the way of gadgets and special trims.

CHAPTER 9

MUSTANG FIGHTS BACK

The problems of the Mustang had not gone unnoticed. As early as the winter of 1969 Lee Iacocca had voiced his concern at the way the Mustang had gone and was still going. He was now Company President of the Ford group and could do something about it. He said: 'All the 1974 Mustang will have to be is one thing. It will have to be a little jewel.'

Iacocca sensed that there was a market waiting for a properly redesigned Mustang, perhaps not the same market that had welcomed its birth, but a large market nonetheless. Depression, recession and rules and regulations had not made the potential market any smaller. It was still there, but it was looking for something appropriate, something small but very well made, something with style and precision and real quality.

As before, Iacocca sparked the designers into interest by staging a design competition, and they responded enthusiastically. Excitement returned, the weight of darkness began to shift.

Research began among the public, who were shown a wide variety of small domestic and foreign cars including Honda, Toyota, Datsun, Opel, Porsche, Triumph GT and Spitfire, MGB GT, Pinto, Vega, Camaro and Plymouth Duster. Included were a trio of fiberglass models of some designs that Ford had created in its codenamed 'Arizona' series. This and other research indicated that people were interested in the sporty-looking subcompacts and in fun-driving that did not necessarily include burning trenches into the local streets. They wanted nimbleness and freshness of handling and design. Most did not care that the rear seats were cramped. Small size was what they wanted.

Other research showed how small foreign cars were still selling well in the US and the success of the Ford Capri was a clear indication of the large market waiting for the right car.

The Arizona program and the Ohio program were set up to design the new car but they had to contend with existing engines and designs like the Pinto. They were trying, in fact, to use existing tooling. The famous Italian design studio of Ghia had been bought out by Ford and Iacocca decided to have them design a new concept. In fact they supplied Iacocca with a totally new working car in 53 days. This achievement acted as a spur to everyone involved, for now they had a car they could drive around in, a new concept they could use as a working example to bounce their own ideas off. The wide-open thinking, most of it unproductive, was sharply focussed by the arrival of the Ghia.

Now the planners clashed with the designers over the engine. The planners wanted them to use the Ford production Straight Six. The designers disagreed. The engine was wrong, it would take the car in the wrong direction, it was too large and the same process of ballooning would begin again. They were out of luck. So Don De La Rossa made a clay around the Straight Six and asked his boss Gene Bordinat to call in Iacocca. Don De La Rossa laid it on the line: a small car had to begin with a small engine; just look what the Straight Six would do to any design. That was the end of the matter, Iacocca agreed. According to Bordinat: 'The next thing we heard was that the choice of engines would be a new small 2.3-liter four-cylinder and a larger displacement version of the German Capri V6, so we were able to get down to making the rest of the car smaller too.'

Iacocca took a keen interest in the growing designs, searching among all the ideas for a car that would be elegant and give the impression of quality and fine engineering.

Public opinion, as relayed by research, showed a neat 50–50 split between notchbacks and fastbacks. This gave rise to a crucial debate about the ultimate shape of the new Mustang. With no clear public preference, it was a problem which shape to choose. Iacocca left it to the three-month long competition between Ford, Lincoln-Mercury, Advanced and

'74 saw the advent of the Mustang II. The elegant precision of the new design earned for it, and for the whole Mustang series, the title of 'Car of the Decade'. Prominent pony emblem, triple rear lights and recessed side panel were unmistakably nostalgic.

Opposite: '73 convertible, the end of a line.
Previous page: '75 Mustang notchback with opera window.

Interior Studios to see what they would do with the problem. Something like 50 clay models were constructed by the competing designers, who all worked to a series of measurements laid down by the engineers, including headroom seating position, reach, sight lines, steering column, wheel positions and so on. Apart from these, and the basic target of producing a smart car for actual production, the four competing studios were left to do as they pleased. As the designing went on, so did the research, on cues thrown up by the competitive sketches and clays. In one of these research clinics, a notchback by De La Rossa's Advanced Studio did so remarkably badly that it was named the *Anaheim* after the place where the clinic had been conducted. Generally notchbacks did not score as well as fastbacks, though the Ghia-inspired notchbacks were noted for their classic lines.

On the final judging day, Lincoln-Mercury studios showed a streamlined design high-peaked over the wheels. Ford Studios and Interior Studios also had fastbacks, but De La Rossa showed his Anaheim notchback, still believing in its elegance of shape.

Iacocca liked the persimmon-colored futuristic Lincoln-Mercury design a lot, and said yes. He had a few objections; the V-shaped beltline had to come up, and the front was wrong. It had to be more Mustang-like to cue the public in to the car. The trial car had brought back the side scoop that had always been a strong Mustang cue and that, too, won Iacocca's approval.

The design was put out to the Feasibility Studio to see if

there were any problems regarding mass production. The Ford and Interior Studios began work on an interior that had in every way to match the style of the design.

So far the design program on the new car had been uncannily similar to that of the original Mustang, with all the same excitement and competition. Now the interior design had to be completed in the short time of 18 months. But history rarely repeats itself exactly. The product planners and researchers decided to run yet another big clinic to discover public opinion and potential demand, and to see how the public would price the new car. At the last minute Iacocca decided to include De La Rossa's notchback. The Ghia design had made an impression on him, as it had on De La Rossa's team, for as someone had remarked, the notchback seemed to move even when it was still. Nat Adamson, the product planner who had been involved with the program from the off, had also wondered if the fastback was a limiting concept if it were the only shape to be made available. The results of the clinic were totally unexpected. The notchback was winning out.

Apart from this result, it was discovered that people were pricing the car at $800 and more over its intended price, exactly what had happened with the first Mustang. And the potential market was estimated at about 400,000.

The notchback was added to the program 16 months before the production starting date and, because of time and money, the design teams had to find ways of adding the notchback roof to the planned fastback body, and of incor-

porating the same door into both designs. But it had happened before, and no doubt it will happen again.

The jewel was coming together, designers and engineers working to make the car perceived value for money, highly elegant, the right size and superbly engineered. It had to have fine fit and finish and exhibit qualities of ride and quietness normally only achieved with big cars loaded with sound insulation and special suspension.

Suspension had always been a problem and in small cars it had tended to transmit both vibration and noise. Mustang engineers Negstad, Kennedy and Nyquist came up with an innovative idea, an isolated subframe on which front suspension and engine were to be mounted. This U-shaped frame took care of the noise and vibration from the engine, and drivetrain and vibration from the road surface, and absorbed it before it could reach the seats and steering wheel. Noise peaks encountered at certain levels of rpm were solved by an expensive but effective retooling of the engine block faces and transmission housing and the inclusion of a larger-diameter driveshaft.

Rubber insulation was widely used and floor soundproofing was achieved by a compound that melted during paint-baking and set again on the floor contours, thereby sealing the floor area.

The new Mustang was to have rack-and-pinion steering with an option power assistance, which would improve the handling to a point of fine precision.

Hundreds of tests were carried out on all these components, many of them totally new, like the isolated subframe, and almost everything was refined and improved.

Redesigned suspension made for an improved ride, front springs were moved down to the lower control arms and the rear shocks were staggered. The isolated subframe, mounted and buffed with extensively-tested rubber elements, controlled noise, vibration and harshness, and these were also helped by 50 percent more chassis insulation and increased front and rear compliance to absorb bump impacts. Front and rear fender systems were enhanced by special absorbers filled with Poly Gel, a gelatinous substance which allowed up to two inches fender contraction before any damage was sustained.

Base engine for the new little car was metric, a 2.3-liter OHC four-cylinder, which was interchangeable with the 2.0-liter now used in other Ford cars. It featured service-free hydraulic valve-lash adjusters and was built with emissions control systems integrated. Until now, these legally-required systems had had to be added on. There was an optional 2.8-liter V6 from Ford Germany. Transmission was four-speed manual with optional three-speed automatic.

Stu Frey, chief car engineer, was given the task of seeing that every part of the new Mustang had workmanship of the highest order. Frey spent time in Europe examining the methods in use, as Iacocca had insisted that his new little jewel be as finely executed as the best European cars. Frey

instituted a program of fine, almost fanatical, attention to the details of finish. It was troublesome and resource-consuming, but Iacocca had already underwritten the costs required. Gene Bordinat claimed, 'This new Mustang was planned as a top-quality job right from the very start. I am not a very enthusiastic fellow, but I think this is the most finely finished automobile that any American manufacturer has ever made.'

The jewel was being polished for display.

Part of the polishing process was for Ford to look again at the 'running horse' emblem and come up with a new look. Among other talents, Charles Keresztes, a Ford designer, was both a horseman and sculptor. He produced a magnificent mustang, straight out of the wide open plains, lovingly sculpted for the new Mustang. Keresztes, under the influence of Frederic Remington, that great painter of the West, also produced a group of mustangs in frolicsome mood. This evoked another Iacocca classic quote: 'I want you guys to know that from now on you're limited to no more than 21 horses per car.' In December 1972 the first '74 prototype was ready for Iacocca to drive. Afterwards, he switched off the engine, chewed his cigar, and said to Gene Bordinat, 'We've got a smash.' From the meticulous Iacocca, that was high praise indeed.

In the seven months before production in July '73 there were a number of small points to finalise — but nothing dramatic, no last-minute panics or management stampede away from the concept.

In order to communicate the fact that the new Mustang was the first of a new generation, it was decided to call it *Mustang II*. This would set it aside from what had immediately preceded it and would state directly that a brand new Mustang was around, something that the description *'74 Mustang* would never do in the same way.

Strangely, it was the original Mustangers who formed the major target market again. They were by now the affluent middle-management types. Ford was still tracking them down and, as in the past, there was an element of risk involved. The ponycar had declined in its share of the total market and, even though the Mustang was the leading ponycar, the idea was to win back the original demographic bulge of those born just after the Second World War. Ponycars of US stock were under attack from foreign imports, and Mustang was under additional pressure from other manufacturers.

Once more the steady build-up of awareness began, with selective leaks, fuzzy photos and leading statements. The idea was to build up interest over a period of time so that everyone would be aware of the new car, so that the idea of it would enter their consciousness in a constant flow. One fear was the possible linking of the economy Pinto with the Mustang II, with a subsequent downgrading in people's minds of the new car. Ford were looking for a repeat of the original Mustang in 1964. It was publicised that the car would do 20 miles per gallon, with a base trim price of under

Extensive research and testing went into the series. It featured an innovative and isolated subframe to eliminate vibration, rack-and-pinion steering and interior sealing.

Previous page: Iacocca's 'Little Jewel'.

$3000. It was estimated that first year sales would be 350,000 units.

But Mustang II was destined to have a bumpier ride than its original. Though press reaction was generally favorable, there was none of the total acclamation of the '64 Mustang. Several writers did not like the little V6 2.3-liter, claiming it was weak for the weight of the new machine. Sales were also adversely affected by the fact that not enough of the base cars were available, and the heavily-optioned models in the showrooms had correspondingly higher price tags, some of them up to $4500. Those people looking for Mustang IIs at the base price of $2895 were disappointed and bought other cars instead. History was not going to repeat itself in the same manner; people were now looking very hard for economy and there was a lot to choose from among the Japanese and European imports. Mustang Mania was a thing of the past and

could not be recreated by any amount of marketing campaigns and merchandising.

Then came the oil embargo in October 1973 and once more people wanted smaller cars. Low sales began to pick up, with the Mustang II competing hard against Vegas, Pintos, Gremlins, Novas, Mavericks and Valiants.

Then President Nixon's wage and price freeze sent prices up on nearly everything. Mustang II was exempt for a while, under anti-inflation rules, and this was to its advantage, though it was not to escape price hikes later in the year. Sales were a very creditable 296,041 despite the gloomy economic scene.

Taking note of the criticism regarding the power of the Mustang II, Ford squeezed a 302 V8 into the car for 1975. Small external changes were supplied, with standard radial tires and solid-state ignition. The luxury end of the range

The front arrangement and recessed side panel revived memories of earlier Mustangs.

In 1977 the Cobra II took up the new theme.

Opposite: King Cobra Model 302.

(entitled 'Ghia') acquired an 'opera window' on its notchback models, plus full or half vinyl roof.

1975 was a tough sales year, with cars being stripped to reduce price tags and dealers offering substantial discounts to shift slow-selling lines. Loaded with rules, regulations, fuel fears, insurance worries, inflation wounds, unemployment and climbing raw material prices, the industry was left staggering. Ford put through a determined program of bringing out higher-mileage versions of all its cars. Power units were modified 2.3-liter four-cylinder engines linked to 3.18:1 rear axles. EPA ratings for the Ford MPG (miles per gallon) program were: highway 34 mpg, city 23 mpg and 30 mpg with manual transmission and 21 mpg with automatic.

Tested against the Monza 262 V8 from Chevy, the V8 Mustang outdid its rival in handling, cornering, acceleration, quarter-miling and braking sensitivity. *Road and Track* magazine, who ran the test, added, 'It is virile in character too, a quality almost totally absent from this year's crop of cars.'

Sales for 1975 were 199,199, dominating the rather slow small car market. For '76 there were catalytic converters and a four-speed manual option for the 302 V8. There were also two appearance packages named 'Stallion' and 'Cobra,' which were aimed at the youth market who wanted to brighten up their cars. The second of these was a cheerful imitation of the old Shelby Mustang transferred to the sub-compact Mustang II. With blue-on-white or black-on-gold, it had stripes, scoops and spoilers. It was sneered at, but gradually made an impression. The idea stuck, and Charlie Kemp, a road racing fan, built a Cobra II-based machine and ran it during the '76 season.

Price increases dogged the 1976 season, putting the base Mustang II up to $3535 and the Mach 1 up to $4209. Sales were down to 178,541 for the model year. But the imitation

Shelby car, the Cobra II package, did better than expected and so Ford took the production into Dearborn from Motortown. They planned more of the same for '78, a package to be called King Cobra, which harped on the spoiler and scoop.

The straight Mustang IIs got options like the Ghia's Sports Group, which consisted of flip-up or removable twin roof hatches and adjustable driver's seat. New standard fitments for the 2-plus-2 fastback were sports steering wheel, styled steel wheels and blacked-out grille. Notchbacks got a new horizontal-bar grille and fastbacks had the Cobra-style chin spoiler available free. Californian drivers, whose State's regulations were the toughest in the land, got a new variable venturi two-barrel carb for both V6 and V8. The venturi openings were worked automatically to ensure steady air-fuel mixing.

Mustang II sales continued to fall in 1977 to 161,654, and the whole '77–'78 turnaround period was hopelessly confused by the failure of Congress to finalize emissions laws, leaving the industry unable legally to produce '78 cars.

The King Cobra arrived in '78 and there was also a Fashion Group of accessories with the female driver in mind. Optional powered rack-and-pinion steering now came with variable ratio and the mileage per gallon from the V6 automatic was slightly increased by a revised torque converter.

To make things more sticky, the Government brought in Corporate Average Fuel Economy rules (CAFE). This meant a manufacturer selling a vehicle below the EPA rating would have to compensate for the mpg shortfall by selling another vehicle with sufficient mpg rating to cover the difference. EPA ratings were to be: 1978, 18 mpg; 1979, 19 mpg; 1980, 20 mpg; 1981, 22 mpg. Increments continued until 1985 when the required figure would be 27.5 mpg. Any manufacturer failing to comply with these stringent fuel economy measures would be in line for a massive cash fine.

CHAPTER 10

THIRD GENERATION

The most up-to-date Mustang was on the cards (and on the drawing boards) more than a year before the launch of the Mustang II. Mustang II was not the total failure that some people claim, for no way would it be possible ever to recreate the dramatic break from tradition represented by the original ponycar. Mustang II served a very important bridging role over some very troubled waters, and could be seen as the car that kept the concept alive until a brand new series was developed. Experience with Mustang II pointed the way forward to a total freshness of design to meet a totally different era. Domestic and international troubles, wars, rumors of wars, oil crises, oil embargoes, price increases, inflation . . . you name it, it happened.

Ford, in common with other manufacturers, always had at the back of its mind the idea, or ideal, of a 'world car' that could be produced all over the world, to meet all the world's requirements. Of course such a thing is not possible. The nearest vehicles that have ever come near it are the Willy's Jeep and the British Landrover, both universal workhorses. Personal transport is something else again. It has to reflect a self-perceived image, it has to comply with vastly different legal requirements, national feelings, road conditions, social contexts. Occasionally a personal car will find wide acceptance, but that is miles away from the idea of a world car.

Yet Ford pushed ahead with its FOX program, to seek a car design that would simplify planning and construction complexity and allow commonality of parts between factories in different countries. Arguably it tried to do too much with existing concepts and existing types — but that is a fact of life in the automotive world. You have to start with what you have in the way of concepts and markets. It was eventually recognized that differing national safety and other requirements would make working from one single design platform a practical nonsense. But Ford were left with a positive attitude regarding compact, fuel-conserving cars and the idea of a single platform serving several different models was to be validated on the domestic market. After all, the original Mustang had itself been almost entirely Falcon-based in components and the Mustang II had relied heavily on Pinto parts. Ford correctly decided that the platform should be Mustang-oriented, but should be capable of supporting other cars as well. In this sense Mustang became the wellspring of the new designs.

Several design directions were pursued at one and the same time, with Gene Bordinat overseeing the work of separate studios and allowing them to do much as they pleased to begin with. Some continued with the old Mustang cues, others did original designs based on European sports design cues. Studios involved were three in Dearborn and one in Turin, where the Ghia studio was now headed by Don De La Rossa. After the decision-spiralling that had taken place on the Mustang II, it was decided that there would be a notch-back first, followed by a fastback. Each studio was given the same hard points, the same dimensions, to work from. Jack Telnack, recently from Ford Europe, had assumed responsibility for North American Light Car and Truck Design and it was his studio that came up with a radically new design

A semi-fastback version repeated the theme of the new front slope.

Previous page: The latest Mustang from the Ford stable, the stylish and efficient SVO Mustang Turbo.

Telnack's '79 design wrapped the fender line into the bodywork, streamlining the shell and giving the wheels a sporty prominence.

Below: The '79 5-liter had new integrated sloping front, recessed oblong lamps — and terrific style.

concept. It had a sloping hood and a slanted nose, a very low beltline and a typically European aerodynamic feel to its shape. Telnack had in fact broken his orders by altering a critical hard point; by changing the height of the cowl his designers were able to slope the hood. This meant new supports for the radiator but it added to the forward visibility and added greatly to the design's aerodynamic qualities and looks. The rear window was aerodynamically wrapped around and the added amount of side glass gave the design lightness and increased visibility.

Telnack's designers added a semi-fastback to their notchback. This made the design popular with both Ford and the research clinics that were being set up to monitor the process. So well was the design received that it went into production virtually unchanged. Louvers were added to the C-pillar and taken away from the grille, which acquired an 'eggcrate' design, and that was all.

The Telnack design was all new. It had none of the old Mustang cues and in that sense was revolutionary, like the original Mustang had been for its time. There were problems when the design reached engineering feasibility stage but the car had such support from management that the engineers were simply told to get on with the job and make it work. There was opposition to the molding of the rear hatchback, solved by managerial insistence. As one designer relates: 'They just stood on those guys and said, "You *will* make the car look like this".'

Telnack's design went into the tunnel and was found to need merely some fine tuning. In fact the wind tunnel tests proved the wisdom of at least one design item that had been disputed, the wraparound rear lights. They had been dis-

Three exciting views of a 1979 5-litre semi-fastback version GT with added air scoops.

puted on traditional grounds as the previous Mustangs had always had flat back panels. Telnack related: 'It was probably one of the first US programs that was so function-oriented, where design decisions were made by the wind tunnel rather than by the whim of the designer or management.'

Intensive mechanical testing followed on a variety of prototypes that were driven to bits to test the new componentry. Apart from component testing, there was crash testing, fender testing, corrosion testing, vibration and noise elimination. There were also long distance evaluation tests and subjective tests to find out those unquantifiable problems that only human experience can detect. The extent of testing was seen in a quote by John Velte, of chassis engineering: '. . . a list of the different kinds of tests for front disk brakes alone takes up six pages of standard typing paper.'

The engineering team's work on the suspension began with the adoption of the exclusive Michelin TRX tire and wheel and went on to develop modified strut shock absorbers, developed after an intensive study of European methods of construction. The 5-liter V8 now ran a single belt take-off system for accessories instead of a previous three-belt system. There was rack-and-pinion steering with optional power assistance and new rear axle assembly. Lightweight materials were extensively used on fenders, suspension arms and the like.

A turbocharging system was introduced late in the program, which meant extensive modifications in the engine to balance the increased heat and backpressure. A two-phase

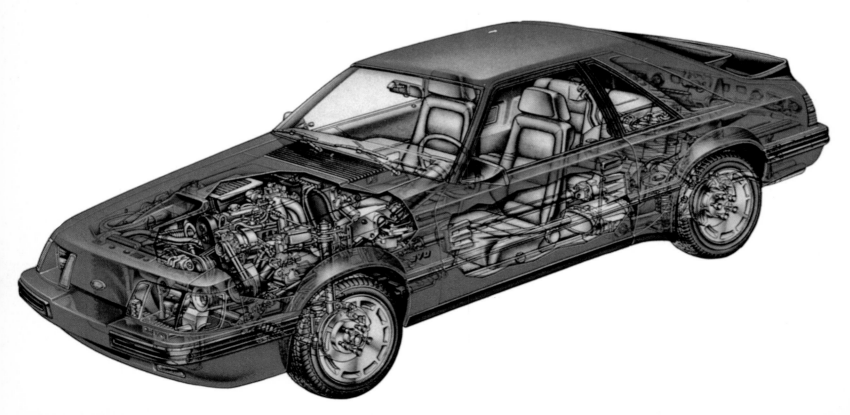

This page: View and cut-away of the '84 Mustang GTP.

Opposite page: View of the '83 Mustang convertible and engineering cut-away of '84 SVO Mustang Turbo.

retardation process was designed, plus a safety valve system. All internal engine parts had to be upgraded to racing standards to cope with the high pressures and temperatures. The turbocharger was a Garret AiResearch unit that gave 20,000 rpm on idle and 110,000 rpm at maximum boost. A predicted 147hp and 154 lb ft of torque were in fact detuned by an overcautious Ford to 132hp and 145 lb ft of torque.

Media stories were balanced between enthusiasm and chin-stroking appreciation of the new car's capabilities, with the TRX coming in for unqualified praise. Best recorded times were 0–60 in 8.3 and the quarter in 12.9 secs.

The new car began selling well, doubling the monthly sales of the old Mustang II, lifting the marque from number 22 to number 7 in the sales charts, and it was chosen to pace the 1979 Indianapolis 500. With scoops, Recaro adjustable seats and a black/pewter color combination with orange-and-red striping,

it had a special 302 V8, aerodynamic spoilers, T-roof and a hood scoop. Introduced at mid-year, approximately 6,000 replicas were built and sold.

The third generation Mustang design was intended to have a long life, so it came as no surprise when, for the second year of its rejuvenation, there were few, and mainly minor, changes. The 1980 Cobra version copied the scoop and spoiler treatment of the Indy pace car, but using a more economical 4.2 liter V8 for power.

Sales figures dropped considerably compared to 1979, but this was to be expected following on from such a bonanza introduction. Problems with the supply of the German-built 2.8 liter V6 caused a change to the domestically produced 200 cu in straight six and the 302 cu in V8 was discontinued, if only temporarily. The 255 cu in replacement rated 119 brake horsepower at 3,800 rpm.

Other engine choices remained as the 140 cu in (2.3 liter) four-cylinder overhead cam in normally aspirated and turbocharged forms. Power output of the fours was 88 BHP at 4,600 rpm for the standard version and a healthy 150 BHP for the turbo.

Transmissions were split—four speed manual for non-turbo four and inline six only, although the six could have overdrive, and you could get an automatic on everything. A 'Special Suspension System' was also available and this included forged aluminum wheels shod with Michelin TRX tires. Intended to look like a convertible (still a couple of years away) one curiosity was the carriage roof option which cost $625.

Coming very late in the 1980 model year was the McLaren Mustang. This expensive (at $25,000) and very limited production (only 250 were made) version contained a host of unusual features—no front grille, large front spoiler set low down, big flares on the fenders, functional hood scoops and special Firestone tires on BBS alloy wheels. Under the exotic skin was a muscular, variable-boost turbocharged engine shoving out a more than respectable 175 horsepower. Not surprisingly, the 1980 McLarens have become for collectors some of the most sought after of the modern Mustangs.

A 1984 GT350 convertible, together with the first Mustang.

CHAPTER 11

TO THE PRESENT

1989 LX 2-door sedan can trace a
ten-year styling history.

A further dip in sales figures for 1981 was merely a reflection of the hard times being felt in the auto industry as a whole. But some significant happenings behind the scenes were to shape the future of this latter day Pony car for several years to come. In September of 1980, Ford's Special Vehicle Operations division was started up with Michael Kranefuss at the helm. Factory-sponsored performance and racing was back! Entrants in various forms of competition got Ford assistance and there was even a turbocharged concept car with ultra wide wheels and IMSA styling that toured around the car show circuit.

However, to the buying public there was apparently little change compared to the previous year's models. Some juggling with transmission availability and a new T-roof option that had two removable tinted glass panels was about it. Thanks to some additional body reinforcements, the T-roof was able to conform to all the required Federal regulations. But if the mixture remained much the same, the price certainly didn't! In common with other Fords, Mustang prices shot up by over 1000 dollars, representing a massive 20 per cent plus hike in some instances.

Big news for 1982 was the return of the 302 cu in (or 5.0 liter, as the factory now chose increasingly to go metric with engine capacities) V8, and this was to increase the number of V8s Ford manufactured for Mustangs by five times compared to 1981. Even so, sales showed a further sharp decline, down by over 30 per cent on '81, the traditional enthusiast's love of the V8 insufficient to stem the tide. The list of engines on offer saw the loss of the turbo four, but the normal 140 cu in (2.3 liter) four, 200 cu in (3.3 liter) straight six and 255 cu in (4.2 liter) V8 were still there.

A new model line-up began with the L as the base, progressed through GL and GLX to the top GT designation which had replaced the Cobra.

Ford ads used the slogan 'The Boss is Back' to publicize the comeback of the 302 and, together with a 356 cfm Motorcraft two-barrel carburetor plus a free-flow exhaust system, power output at 157 BHP at 4,200 rpm was enough to give impressive 0–60 mph times of under eight seconds.

A true Mustang convertible at last reappeared as part of the 1983 GLX range and racked up sales of over 23,000. Convertibles were not actually built by the Dearborn factory;

instead, assembled two-door notchbacks were shipped to Cars and Concepts in Brighton, Michigan, where the top and interior trim were installed. Notch and hatchback styles stayed much the same although all '83 models had revamped noses and rear ends which helped aerodynamically. Headlamps became more recessed and the narrower grille tapered inwards a fraction top to bottom.

Available powerplants were again shuffled around. Gone were the 3.3 liter straight six and the 4.2 liter V8, to be replaced in part by a newcomer, the 3.8 liter (232 cu in) 'Essex' V6. The 302 (5.0 liter) High Output V8 got a single Holley four-barrel carb and aluminum intake manifold which saw horsepower bumped to 175 from 157. Reported 0–60 mph times for the Mustange GT were in the seven second bracket, which put it as the quickest of any standard US model in production that year. Combined with excellent handling characteristics developed from larger sized tires, stiffer anti-roll bars, uprated springs and shock absorbers, together with fuel economy figures around 25 mpg, the '83 Mustang represented an extremely attractive package.

If 1983 was a good year, then 1984 was even better. The establishment of the Special Vehicle Operation a few years earlier showed itself in the Mustang SVO coupé that won rave reviews from the motoring press. *Road and Track* said 'This may be the best all-round car for the enthusiast driver ever produced by the US industry' and *Motor Trend* called it 'the best driving Mustang the factory has ever produced'—high praise indeed.

SVO Mustangs came with an electronic fuel injected, turbocharged and intercooled 2.3 liter OHC four-cylinder that pumped out 175 horsepower at 4,400 rpm and raw excitement! A Borg-Warner T5 manual gearbox and a 3.45:1 ratio in the Traction-Lok rear axle made 0–60 mph claims of 7.5 seconds seem realistic, while the overdrive fifth gear put a top speed of 134 mph within reach—no wonder the journalists were so ecstatic.

Styling of the SVO was as special as the performance—a slot in place of the normal grille, hood scoop, single instead of dual rectangular headlamps, twin wing rear spoiler and spats in front of the rear wheel arches. Available in only four colors (black, silver metallic, dark charcoal metallic and medium canyon red glow) it came with just six options as everything else (more or less) was standard.

The SVO sat almost 1½ inches lower than other Mustangs, had gas-filled adjustable Koni shocks and power-assisted disk brakes all round, and rolled on cast aluminum wheels 16 inches in diameter by 7 inches wide, fitted with low profile P225/50VR16 Goodyear NCT tires.

Price tag for all this excitement was a hefty $15,596, over twice that of a basic L model, putting it firmly in a bracket with the more expensive imported European performance cars, where it could more than handle the opposition!

Back with the more mundane Mustangs, convertibles were now offered in LX and GT forms, while the L could be had in both three-door hatchback and two-door notchback configurations. The GL and GLX model denominations of previous years were combined to form the LX range.

Left: SVO gained plaudits from all the major auto magazines in 1984, with *Car and Driver* calling it 'a Mustang with a mission'.

Above: The tail end of the '84 SVO looked extremely businesslike.

But apart from the SVO, Mustang performance seekers also had the much cheaper GT and Turbo GT models to consider. The GT came with a 5.0 liter High Output V8, either with fuel injection and overdrive automatic or a single Holley four-barrel carb and five-speed manual gearbox as two distinct and separate combinations. GT Turbo models had the same 2.3 liter four as the SVO but without the intercooler, and consequently 30 less horsepower. Either of the hard top three-door GTs was priced below 10,000 dollars, so it was not surprising that they came in for a lot of attention from potential purchasers.

Optional on the L and standard on the LX convertible was the 3.8 liter EFI V6 which, thanks to the introduction of fuel injection, now put out some 120 horsepower, eight more than the preceding carburated unit.

Sales for 1984 picked up somewhat, not surprising perhaps with such positive test reports abounding, thus reversing the trend set since the initial fillip provided by the introduction of the third generation design in 1979. Around 16,000 more Mustangs were produced and sold this year, the total easily exceeding 130,000.

It was all happening up front for 1985, as the whole range virtually adopted the SVO look from '84. Gone was the tapered grille with its rectangular grid, and replacing it was a single large slot. But apart from that and a few cosmetic and trim alterations, the general overall appearance looked little changed.

Behind the Ford oval on the sloping front panel, powerplant choices were also more or less as before: 2.3 liter OHC four in normal and turbo forms, 3.8 liter fuel injected V6 and 5.0 liter HO V8 with either four-barrel carb or EFI.

Above left: Mustang L from '84 with optional cast aluminum wheels and TRX tires would be ordered with V8 engine later in model year.

Above: The small block Ford V8 is destined to power the Mustang into the 1990's; in 1984 it was available as an option and designated as the 5.0 liter HO (High Output) V8.

Left: '84 LX was one step up from the basic L model, but had a wide range of options to allow the buyer to specify the car to suit his or her pocket.

The 1985 GT proved to a lot of people that the V8 still had a part to play in the future of the Mustang. Now boasting a vigorous 210 horsepower, the carbureted small block proved more tractable than the turbo four in day-to-day driving circumstances, delivering so much torque it reminded some commentators of the earlier sixties models. The three-door hatch GT was also over 4,500 dollars less than the equivalent SVO for the second year running, which no doubt added considerably to its appeal.

The LX was now the lowest specification model following the

deletion of the L from the catalog. The two-door notchback was confined to the LX range, but both GT and LX convertibles were still offered. Usually called coupés by customers, three-door hatchbacks went across the board, but SVO was only available in this body shape as before.

Main picture: All '85 Mustangs adopted the smoother front end of the 1984 SVO – this is '85 SVO.

Main exterior changes for 1986 focused on the high-level rear brake light now required thanks to new legislation. In an unchanged range, the LX notch (now called a two-door sedan by Ford) had this addition fixed to the parcel shelf, while the LX hatch won a spoiler to incorporate it. GT and SVO models had a similar spoiler mounting, while convertibles gained a luggage rack that included the new lamp.

Although the '86 engines remained ostensibly the same as before, there was one notable departure. The four-barrel carburetor was no more, replaced by the more efficient sequential electronic multi-port fuel injection, and ending a reign that stretched right back to the very beginning (admittedly with a few gaps along the way). Identical 200 horsepower outputs were obtained from the 5.0 liter EFI V8 and the 2.3 liter turbo four, giving the smaller-engined car lively performance that just about equated acceleration times of the big cube V8 engines of old.

Still soldiering on, giving the same 88 horsepower as ever, the ordinary 2.3 liter OHC four stayed as the base engine. But four cylinders of both types were popular, selling more than 107,000 units, which was more than the V6 and V8 totals combined. In fact, Mustang was a popular car again, sales increased again (the only Ford model that did) and well over 200,000 were produced.

Left: 1986 Mustang GT interior in
Canyon Red trim.

Above: A 200 horsepower
turbocharged 2.3 liter four-cylinder
engine powered the '86 SVO.

Below: LX 2-door sedan was the base
model in the '86 range.

European styling trends filtered through to the Mustang for 1987, particularly on the GT which with the longer, lower hood line grew a much more pronounced front air dam containing a longer opening under the front fender and recessed round driving lights on either side. Side skirts, or 'integrated fender extensions' as the sales brochure describes them, with small air scoops in front of the wheels and a deeper rear panel complete with peculiar 'louver effect' rear lights, added to the new look. The wide slot in the front panel was filled in and headlamps became flush, as did the rear quarter glass for better air flow. As with the majority of modern cars, this streamlining gave the Mustang a much more rounded appearance altogether, but could not quite make it as anonymous as some makes have become.

Now, with the departure of the SVO, Mustang aficionados were left with just the LX and GT to choose from. With the SVO went the turbo four, and the V6 was also discontinued. It was 5.0 liter EFI V8 or 2.3 liter EFI four from now on. But if the choice was limited at least the power from the V8 wasn't—up to 225 horsepower at 4,000 rpm together with even more torque (320 lb ft at 3,200 rpm).

Changes to the LX styling naturally followed the GT, but without all the fancy add-ons, and instead of a flat front panel the Ford oval 'floated' in an opening supported by a thin horizontal bar. 'Mustang' was molded into the bumper below this opening and there were no driving lights.

Below left: Aggressive stance of '87 GT Hatchback told you that here was a car that meant business.

Left: Highly visible feature of the '87 GT was the curious 'lower effect' rear lights.

Above: Engine bay of 1987 GT.

Bottom: 1987 GT convertible simply exudes performance.

Changes in 1988 were minimal and rumors began to circulate that the Mustang name was to be transferred to a front-wheel drive model using Mazda mechanical components under a Ford skin. Whether the subsequent outcry from Mustang enthusiasts caused any change in policy is difficult to ascertain, but it is more likely to have been the fact that '88s were selling well, in excess of 200,000, and no manufacturer would risk losing those sort of numbers. Anyway, the new car was produced as the Probe and the third generation Mustang lived on to celebrate its tenth birthday.

Along the way, the '88 collected some plaudits of its own, particularly from *Hot Rod* which bestowed its 'Best Performance Car of '88' award on the LX with the 5.0 liter V8. 'There is only one car on the market today that offers performance at a truly affordable price' was how part of the citation read. Tests of this combo revealed that low 14-second quarter miles were attainable off the showroom floor, with terminal speeds approaching 100 mph. Still good after all these years!

April 17 1989 was the date that Ford marked as the 25th anniversary of the Mustang, and for '89 production proceeded unabated and unchanged—after all why mess with success? Ford had intended to offer a limited edition model to commemorate the landmark, but corporate indecision and lack of production capacity seem to have killed the idea. Enter Steve Saleen of Saleen Autosport in Anaheim, California, and the Mustang Saleen Super Car (SSC). Saleen races Mustangs in the SCCA Showroom Stock Professional Series and has been involved with Ford since the early days of SVO in 1981, building many hundreds of modified cars in the process.

The SSC is a race-refined Mustang featuring a range of engine modifications designed to push power output close to 300 hp. A unique, all-electronic suspension, with three-position switching from Monroe and 245/50-16. Z-rated General tires mounted on 8 × 16-inch five-spoke wheels painted to match the snow white body (the only color offered), are just a taste of the mouthwatering specification.

Of course, other special Mustangs are produced across America, and have been as long as there have been Mustangs. A typical example is ASC Inc of Southgate, Michigan, and its 1989 ASC/McLaren Limited Edition based on the convertible. A package of front and rear spoilers, molded in side skirts and special wheels, is used to give a different look to a popular car.

One major event that certainly celebrated the 25th anniversary in style was the American Pony Drive when large numbers of Mustang owners from America joined with a caravan of European drivers traveling across the country. In a spectacle unlikely to be equalled for a long, long time it served to demonstrate the feelings of tremendous loyalty and affection generated by the car that started a revolution in attitudes.

In recent times, much of Ford's performance effort has been lavished on the Thunderbird and now the new Probe appears to be grabbing the limelight, so where does that leave the Mustang? A new V8-powered, rear-wheel drive design is promised in the early 1990's and the current version is still at the forefront, offering excellent performance and outstanding value. We can only hope that 'Performance' and 'Mustang' will remain synonymous for another 25 years! The news that Ford, starting in 1989, plans a powerful assault on the Trans-Am championship, is more than reassuring.

1988 Mustangs kept to the now familiar model choices; shown is the LX.

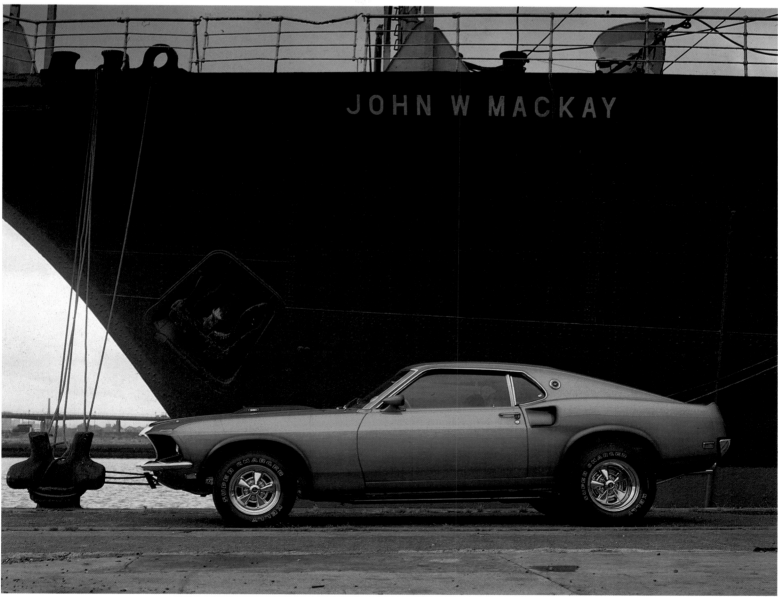

This British owned 1969 Mark 1 is really flawless and has won many show awards.
It illustrates the amount of work some Mustang owners will lavish on their steeds.

CHAPTER 12

MUSTANGS OVERSEAS

Ever since its introduction, the Mustang has found favor in many other countries around the world. In Europe especially, Ford's sporty 2+2 was much sought after in the early days, the combination of styling and performance together with a relatively cheap price finding an enthusiastic audience.

However, as Mustangs changed, so did the foreign buying public. The bulky heavyweights of the early Seventies fell from favor abroad in a fashion similar to that of the home market, but the coming of the compact Mustang II did little for the European driver. After all, his own country's manufacturers had been producing similar vehicles for decades, and doing it a whole lot better when considered in terms of road holding and fuel economy. Americans might have looked on the down-sized Mustangs as something new and appealing, but on the other side of the Atlantic the cry was for V8 performance and distinctive style—that was where for them the appeal of American automobiles had always been—and why buy something that did not have either the blinding acceleration or the muscular looks to distinguish it from all the crowds of run-of-the-mill cars on the road?

With the coming of the Eighties and the new generation of Mustangs, the tide turned to a small degree, but it is fair to say that in a lot of countries, given the choice, the enthusiast will almost always opt for an early model example. However, the retention of the V8 engine and a design that, despite attempts to 'Europeanize' it, still manages to look attractive, yet at the same time different enough to be noticeable, has seen interest in the modern Mustang increase, if only slightly compared to the Sixties. A weak dollar has also helped to keep prices outside the USA very competitive with European domestic products, even allowing for the shipping costs and import duties that have to be added to the purchase price.

Ford USA have shown no inclination to mount a transatlantic export drive, which means that practically every Mustang that appears in Europe these days is the result of a personal import. The problems associated with this method of buying a car (new or used) have restricted exports in recent times to a relatively small number. But what is 'small potatoes' to a giant corporation is often a profitable business opportunity to a small company with only one or two employees, and imports of Mustangs (as well as many other makes and models) have been booming over the past three or four years, with sometimes as many as 300 cars per month arriving at the ports of entry.

Undoubtedly another drawback to the direct export of brand new Mustangs from the factory is the complex regulations that exist in Europe and the way these differ (and sometimes directly conflict) with US requirements. However, California is notorious for imposing special restrictions on the automobiles sold in that state, and the manufacturers manage to cope with these impositions. Other major American automobile makers (notably GM) have shown that they can produce models to suit the export markets, but due to the small numbers anticipated it has tended to be with models at the luxury end of the sales spectrum.

The start of 'The American Pony Drive' where Mustangs from all over Europe did a tour of the USA to celebrate the 25-year anniversary. Models of all shapes and sizes entered this drive of a lifetime.

1967 Shelby GT 500 with 428 cu in, 355 BHP engine produced low, low 14 second quarter miles and a top speed of 130mph. This British owned car is an early one of the 2,050 produced — evidenced by close together spotlamps in front grille, as some States outlawed these and later produced models had them spread wider apart. Full width rear tail lights and extensive fiberglass panels and scoops are other Shelby changes to the base Mustang.

Ford of England did import a 1984 Mustang GT convertible as an experiment—chiefly to give British motoring journalists the opportunity to compare it with the home-produced Ford products being offered to the public. Reaction generally was pretty favorable, although there were one or two anomalies that some testers felt would have to be changed before the car could be sold (even in very small quantities) in the UK.

One such criticism centered on the maximum 85 mph reading on the speedometer, which plainly made little sense to European eyes (especially when the rev counter registered a lazy 2,300 rpm in fifth gear at this speed) and particularly in countries like Germany which had no limit on their famous high-speed autobahns. Other niggles illustrate precisely the task facing a manufacturer who wants to build one model of car for a world market. American drivers (more used to automatic transmissions) could accept a device where the clutch pedal has to be depressed before the engine can be started on a manual gearbox as a safety measure, whereas Europeans regard this as totally unnecessary and awkward and a button, hidden away in the glovebox, to open the fuel filler flap has little relevance in a country where self-service filling stations are the norm.

Poor fuel economy figures (well under 20 miles per *Imperial* gallon were experienced by test drivers) were seen as a big drawback, although it was said that the experience of V8 torque and the ability to chirp the rear tires at will would be more than enough compensation for many potential buyers.

On a more positive note, the handling characteristics of the '84 GT were found to be very much up to par and a great improvement on previous Mustangs. Whether there was ever a serious intent on Ford's behalf to start up imports into the UK again is not clear, but nothing happened and there are no current indications to suggest that this attitude will change.

As the trend of most modern American automobiles continues to approach the European and Japanese ideas of size, styling and engineering, chances have opened up for companies outside the USA to introduce products that previously would not have been acceptable. Typical of these are the bolt-on 'body styling kits' which with their deepened side skirts and dramatic extra front and rear spoilers give a performance and almost 'race car' look, that have proved very popular. Also, many European-designed and manufactured alloy wheels have encroached on a market previously dominated by US producers and can be seen rolling down the freeways. Latterday Mustangs have been ripe for these treatments because of the enthusiasm of the drivers they attract.

Right: 1984 GT 350 convertible was quite a car. British journalists tested a similar car and comments were generally favorable.

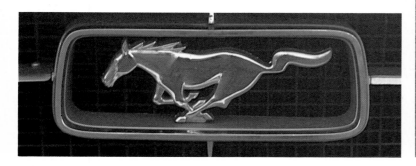

INDEX

Acknowledgments
The Publishers acknowledge with thanks the help received in the provision of the following illustrations: Nick Wright/National Motor Museum for pages 102–3 (below), 105 (above), 107 (above), and 118–9; the Ford Motor Company for pages 96–7, 98–9, 100–1, 102–3 (above), 104 (above), 104–5 (below), 106 (above), 106 (below), 107 (below), 108–9, 112–3; the Editor of *Street Machine* for pages 110, 111, 116, 117, and 120–1; and Andy Willsheer for pages 114–5 and 118 (left).

1984 GT convertible was imported into the UK by Ford for comparison with local automobiles.